To all the dreamers, believers, and adventurers – may the enchanting world of "Enchanted Fairyland" inspire you to color your dreams and paint your imagination with the brightest of hues. Let the magic within these pages remind you that anything is possible when you believe in the power of creativity. This book is dedicated to the spark of wonder that resides in every child's heart.

Cris Cardoso

2024

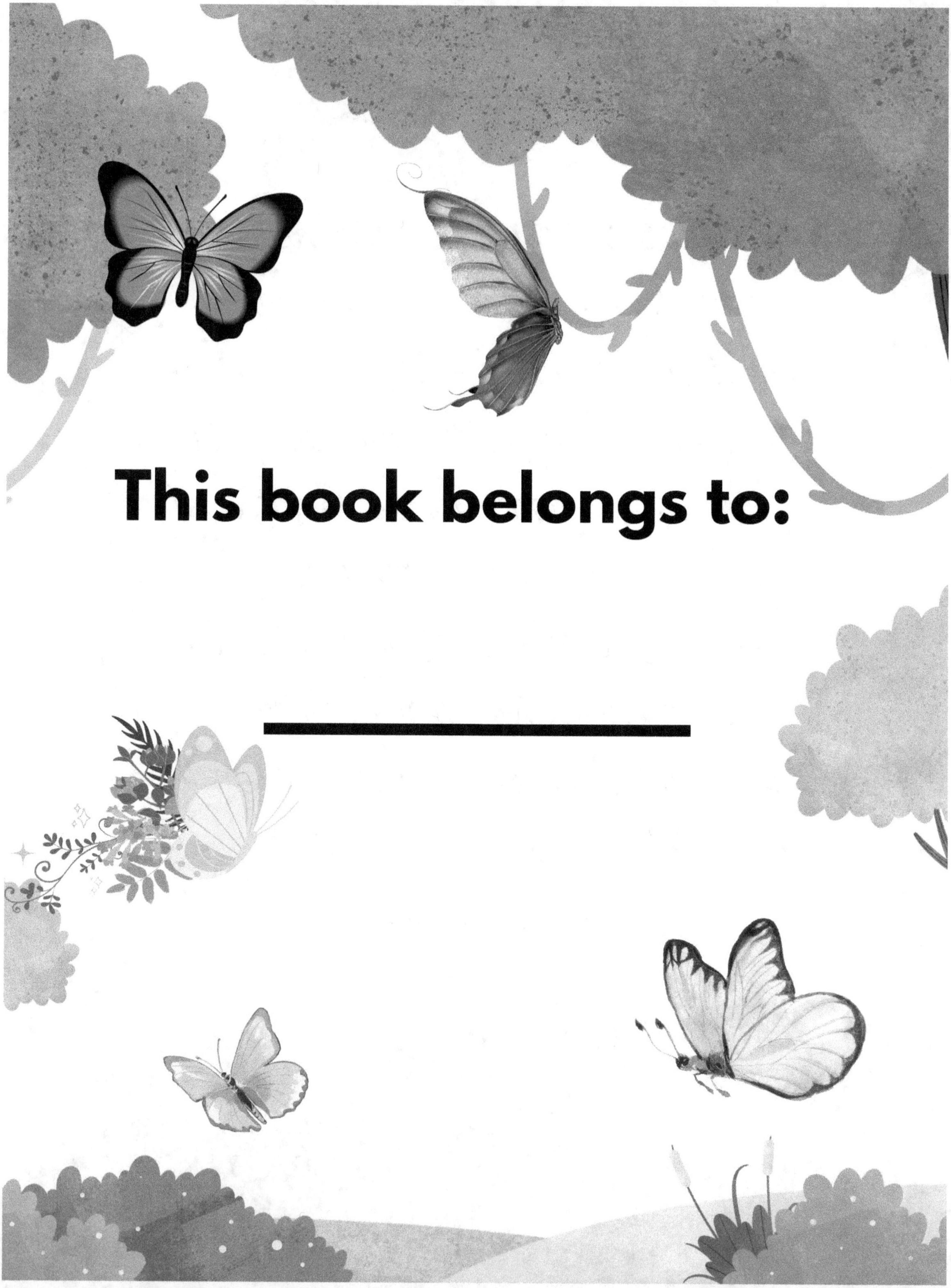

This book belongs to:

_____

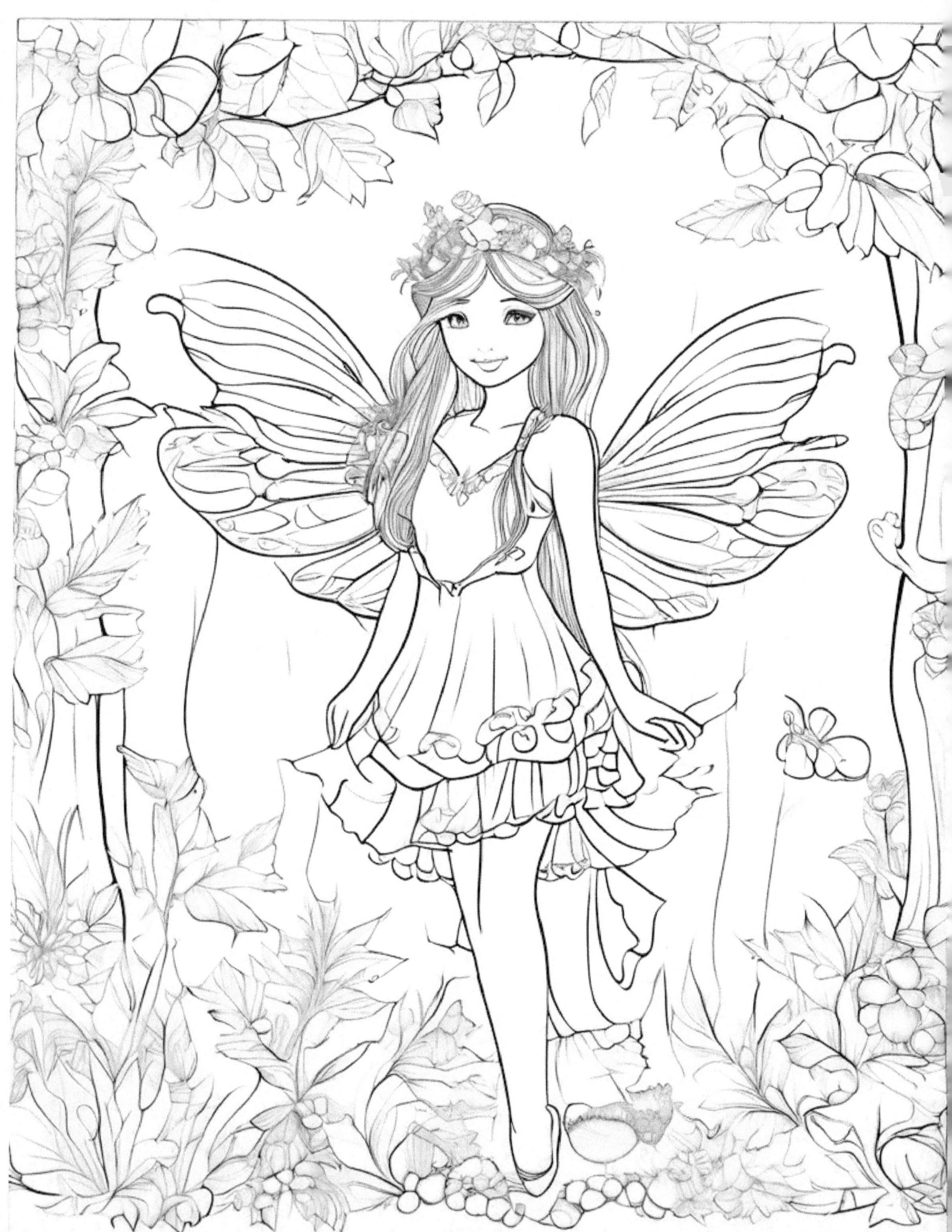

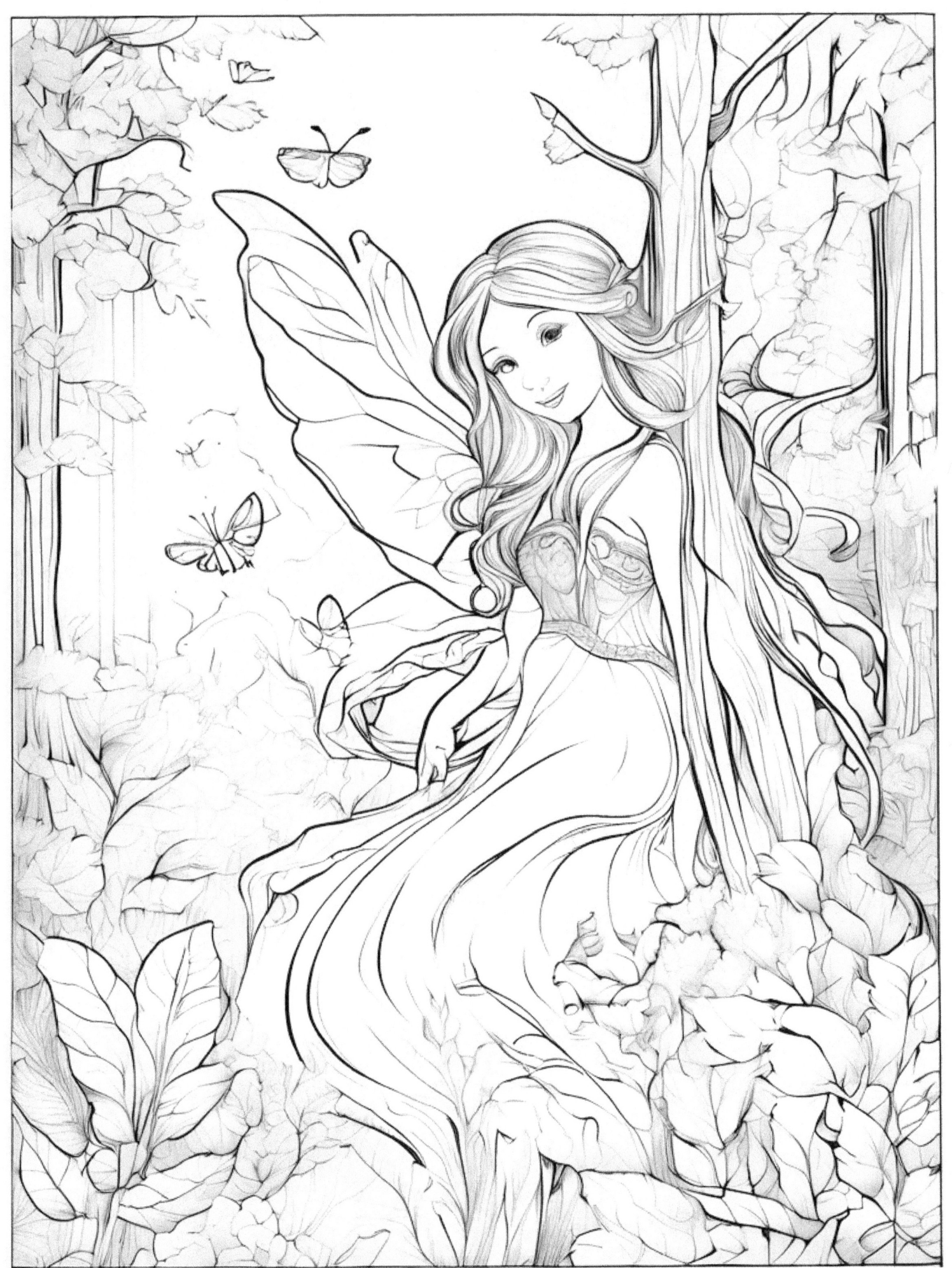

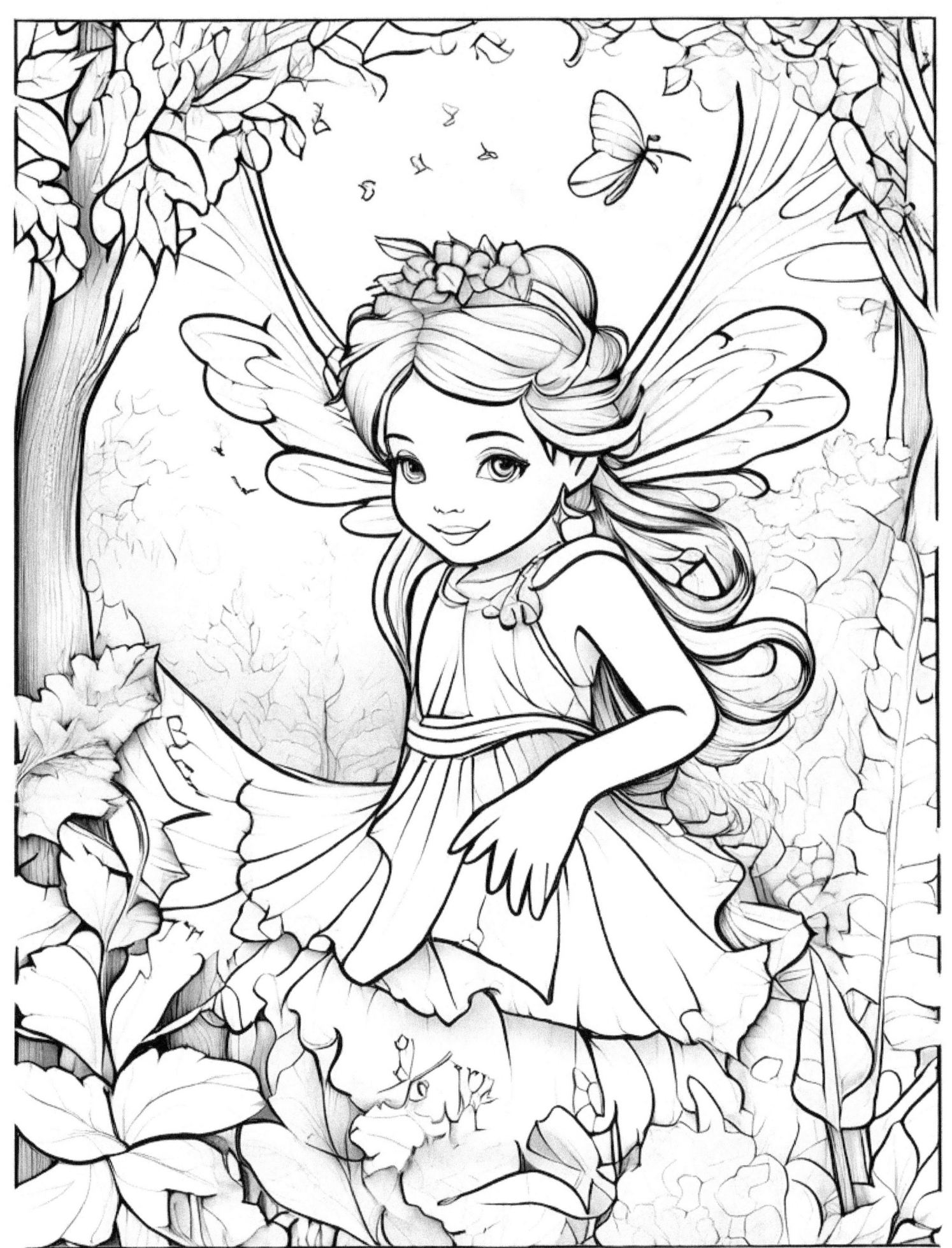

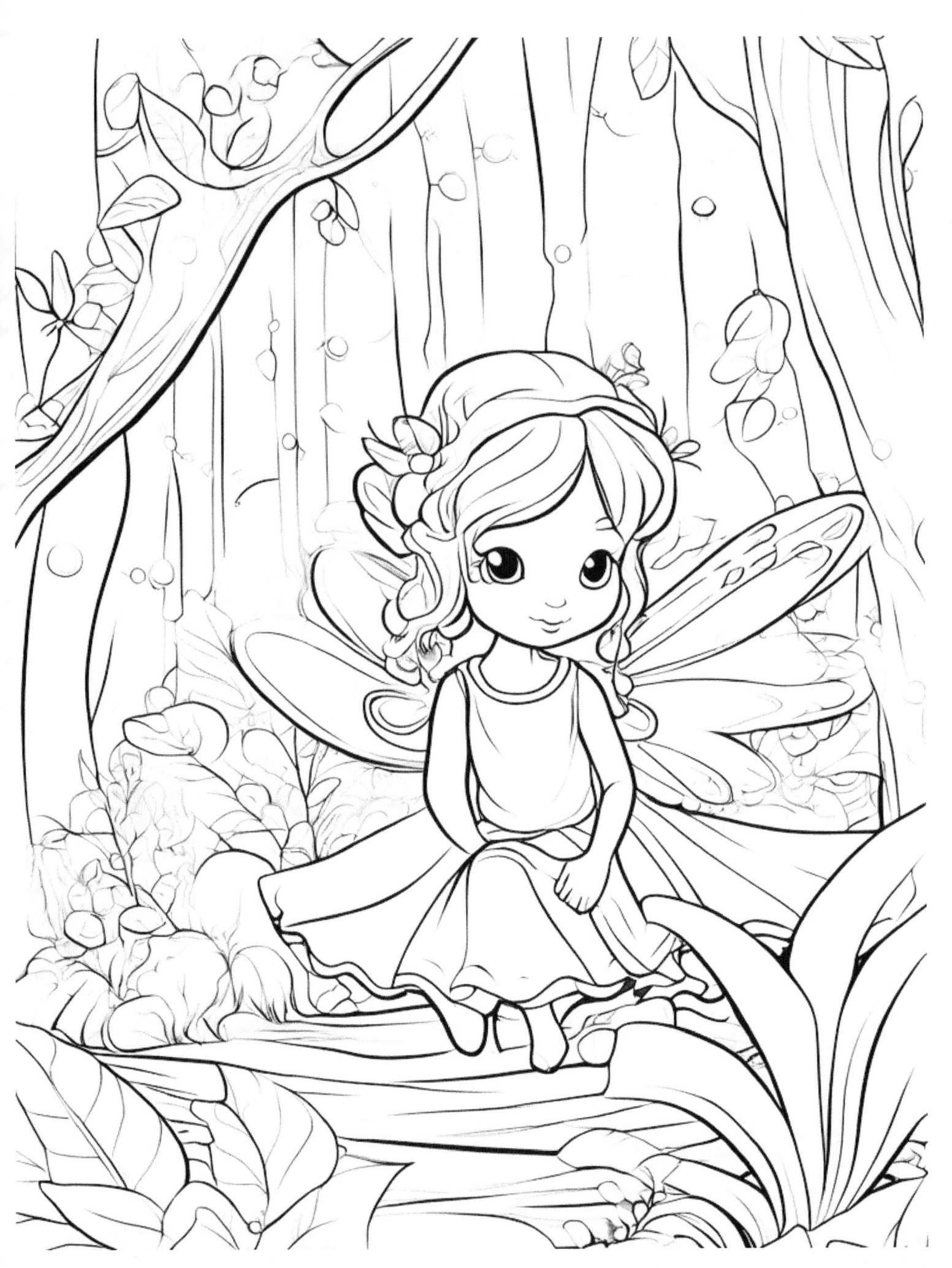

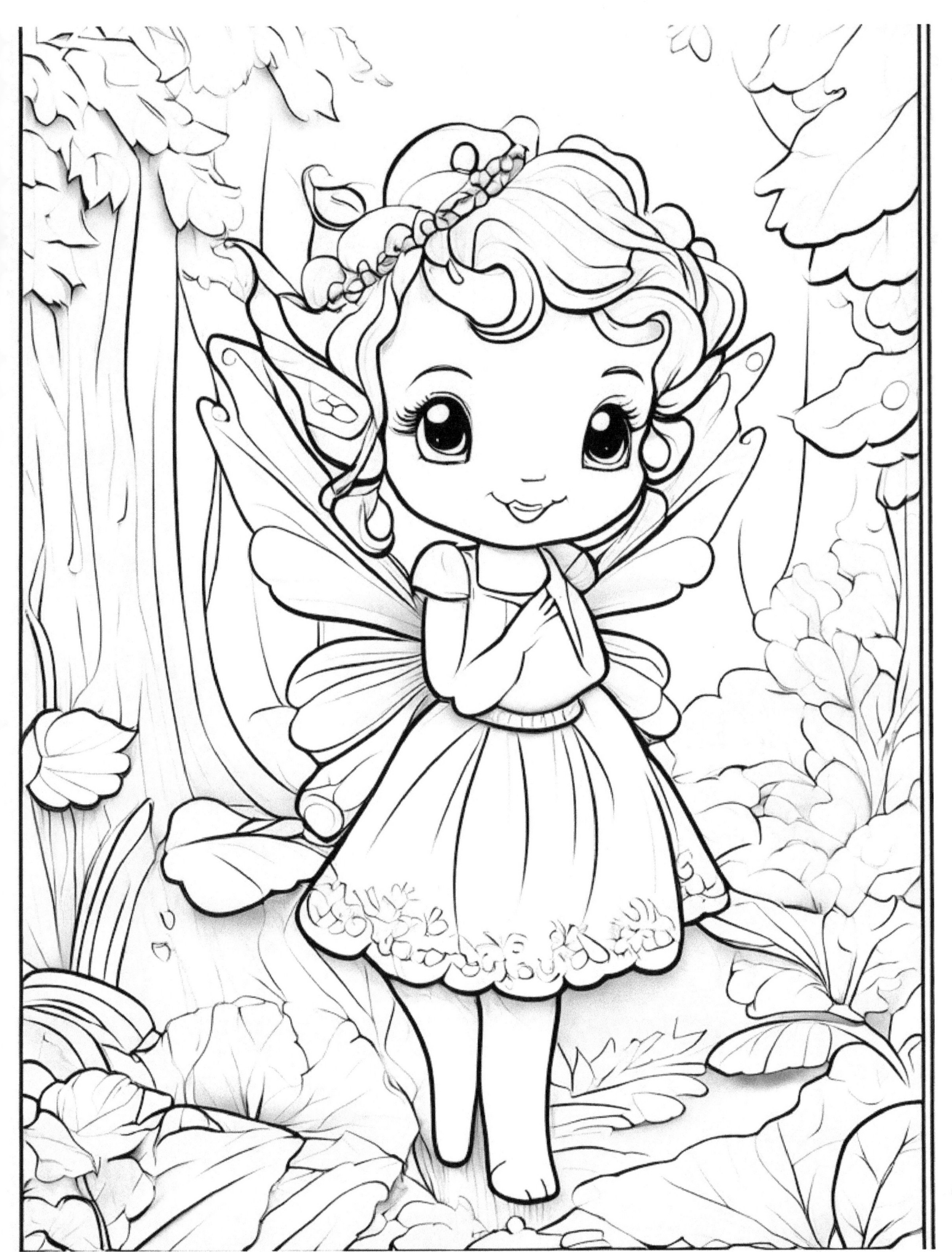

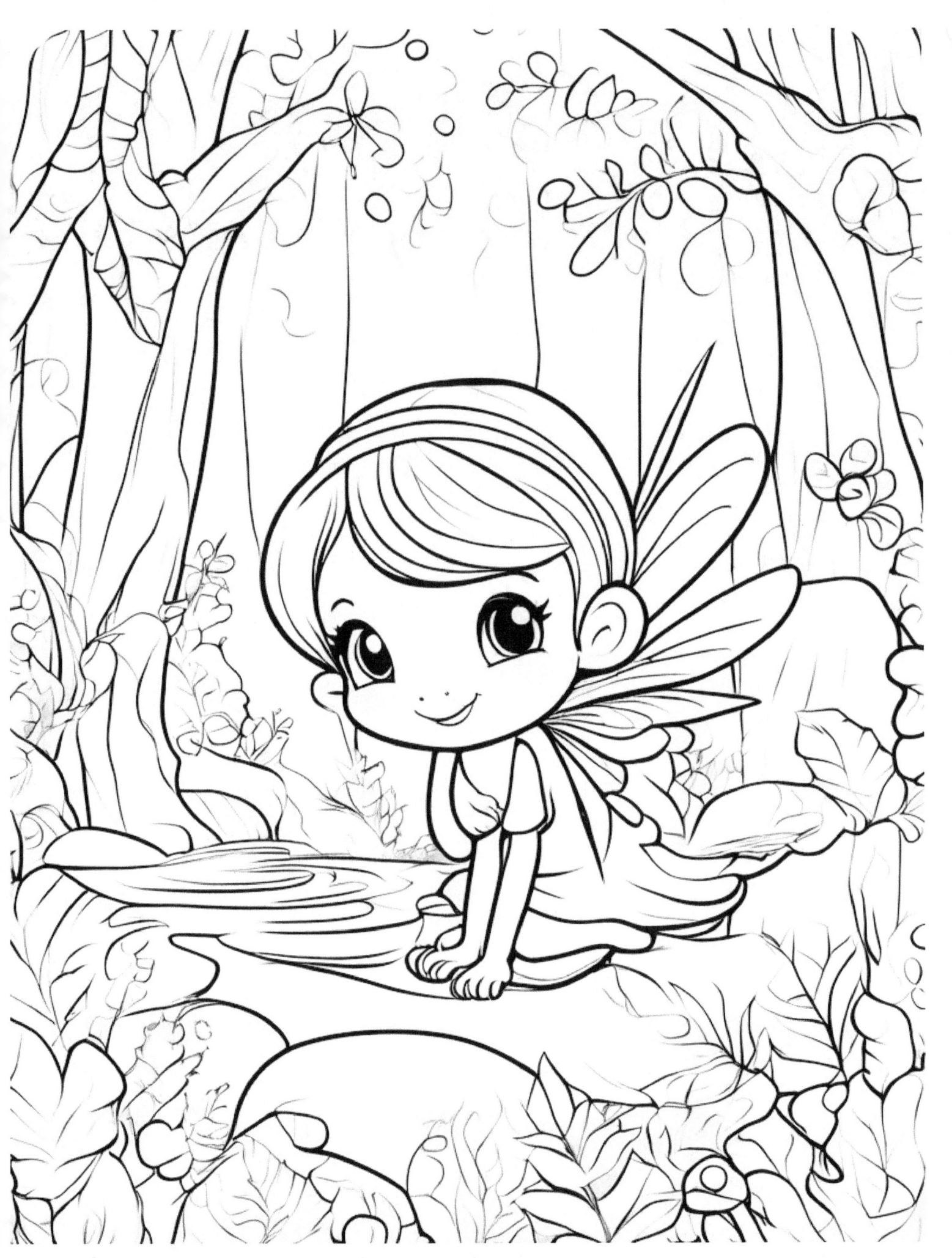

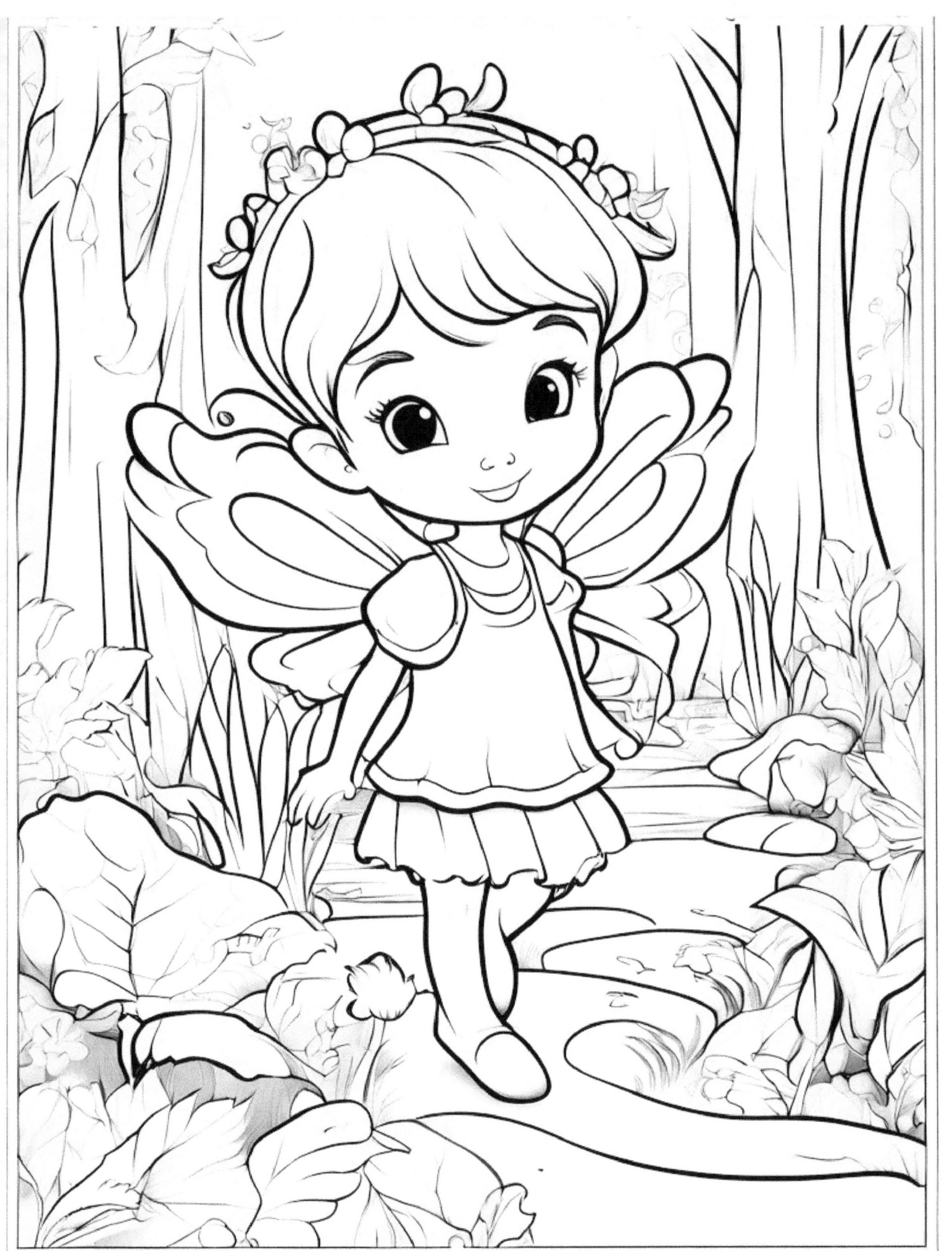

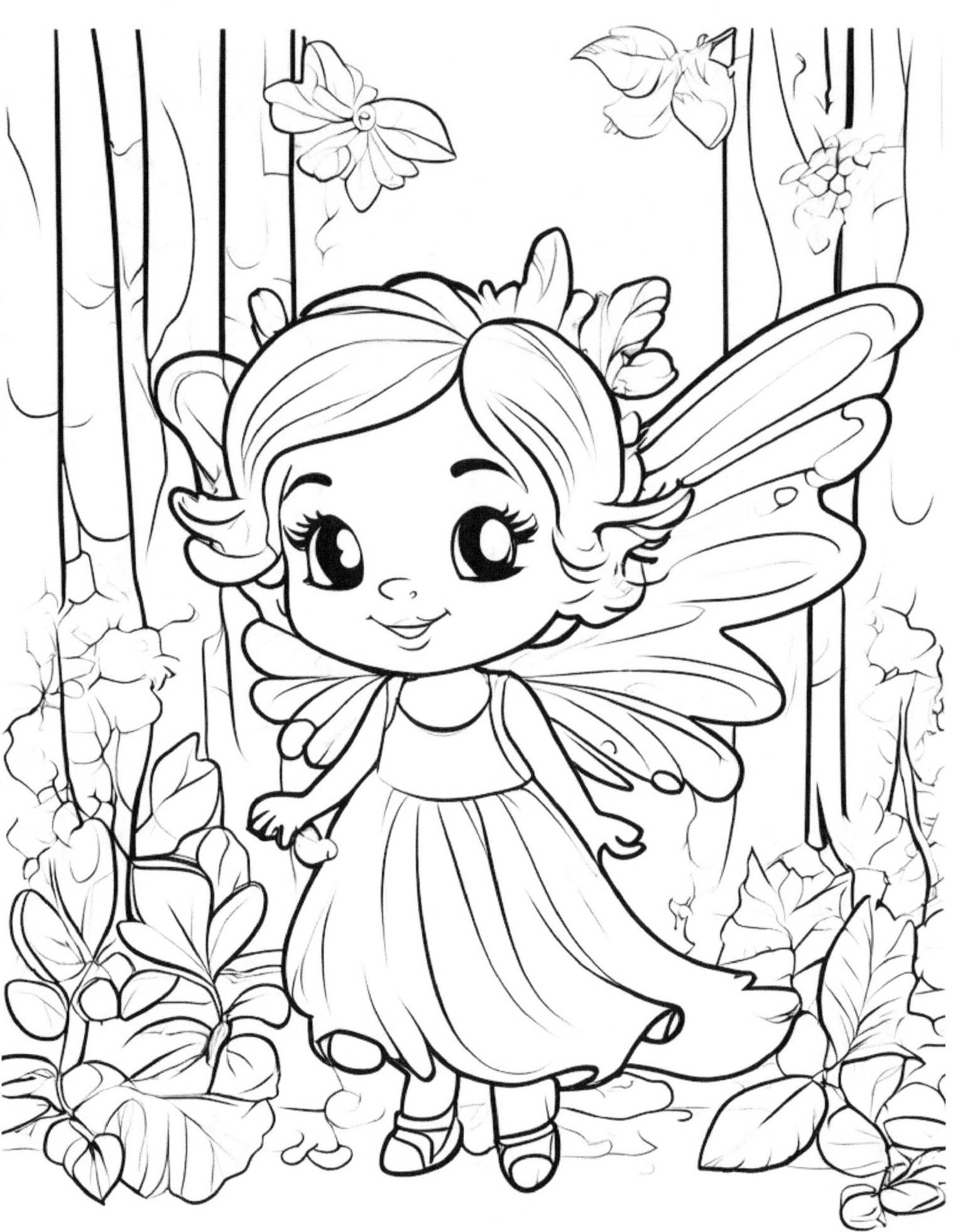

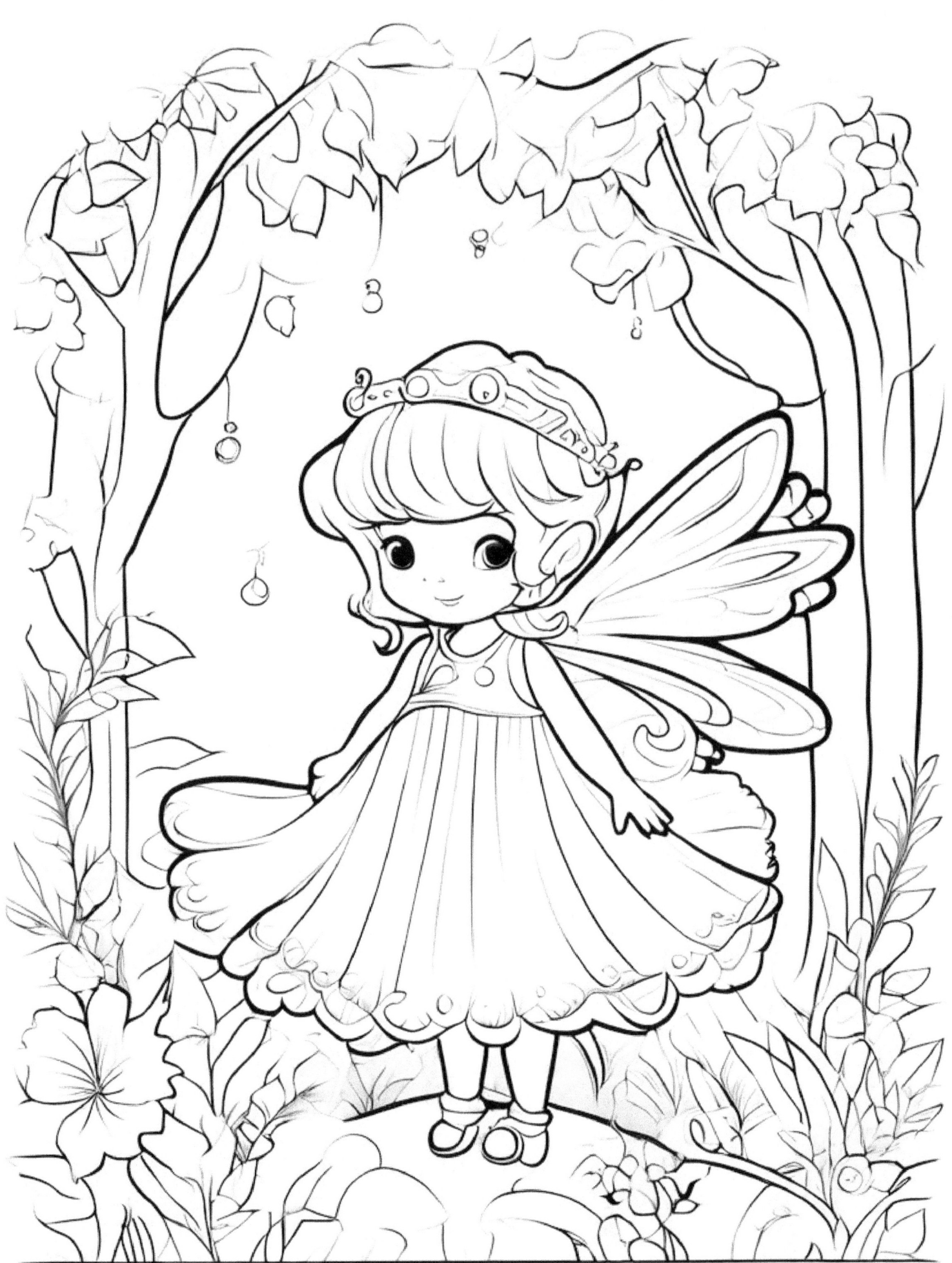

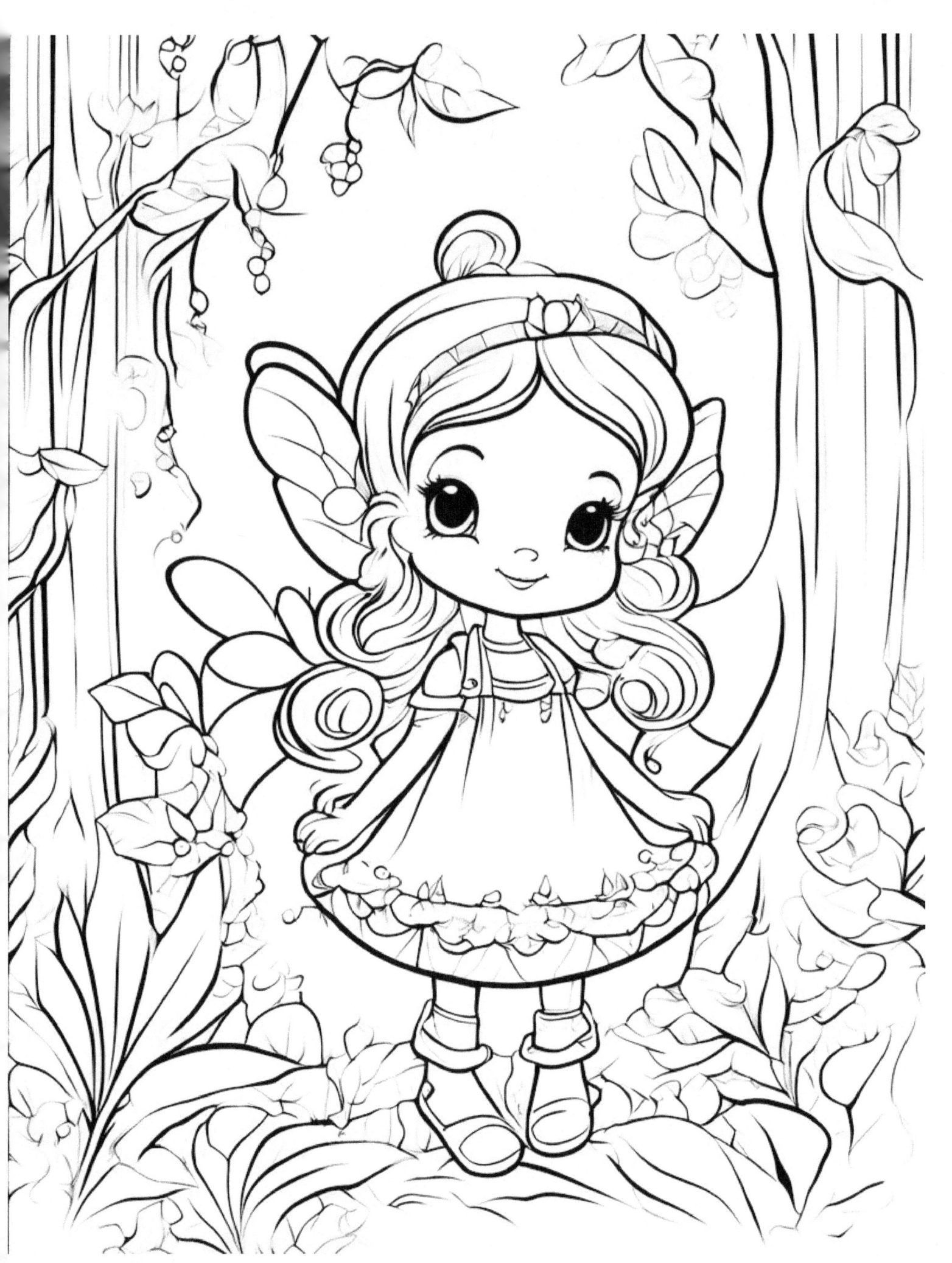

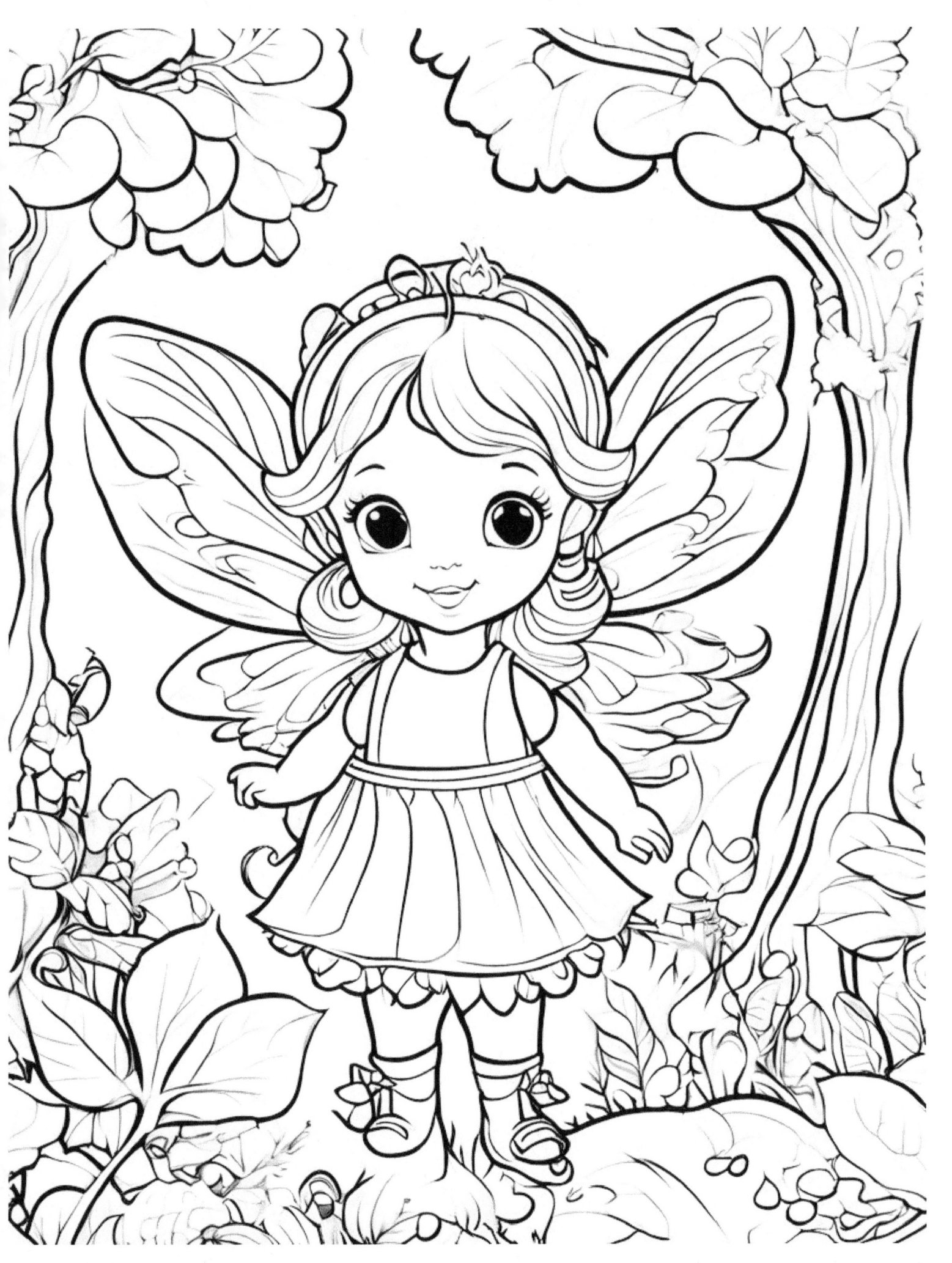

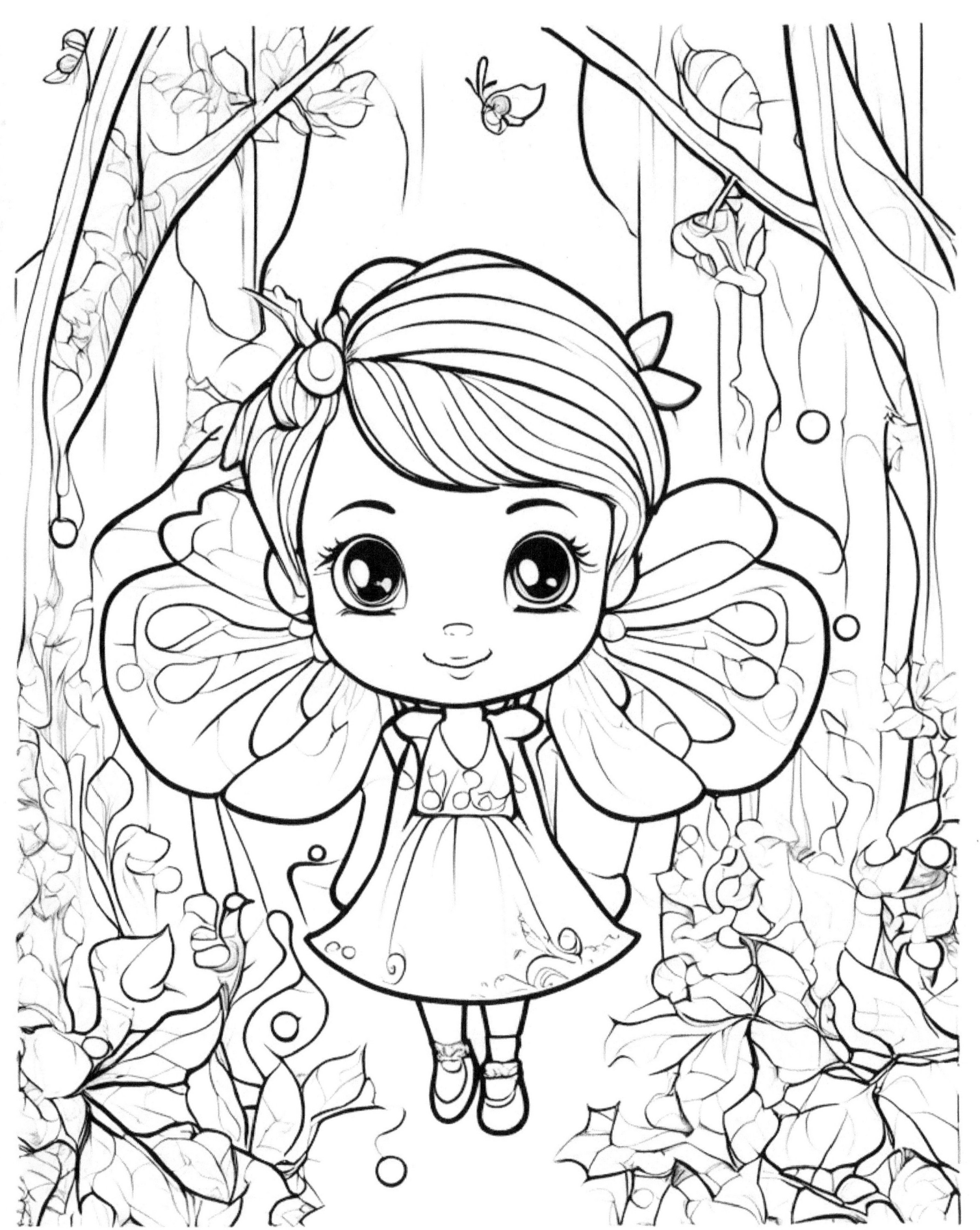

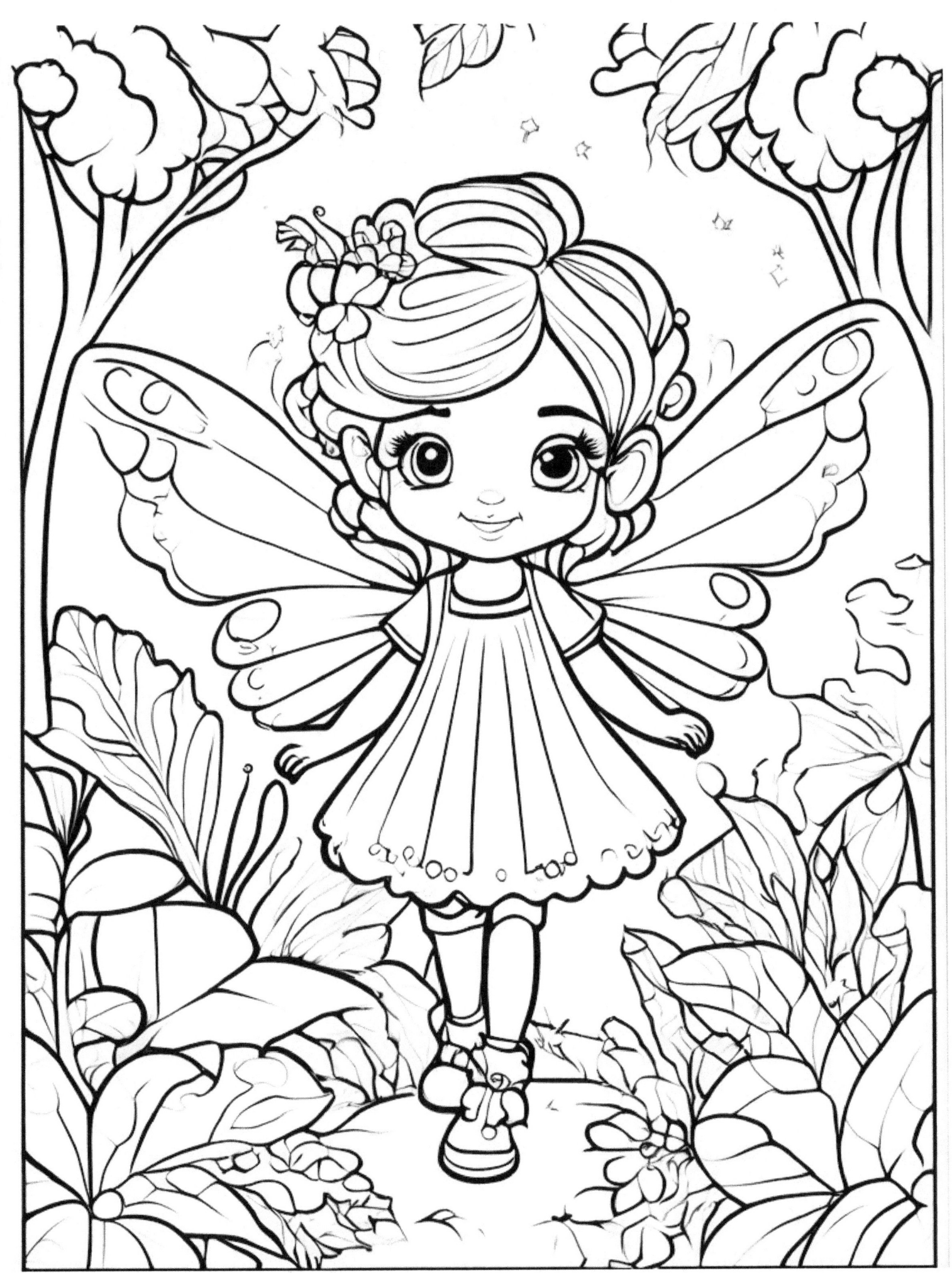

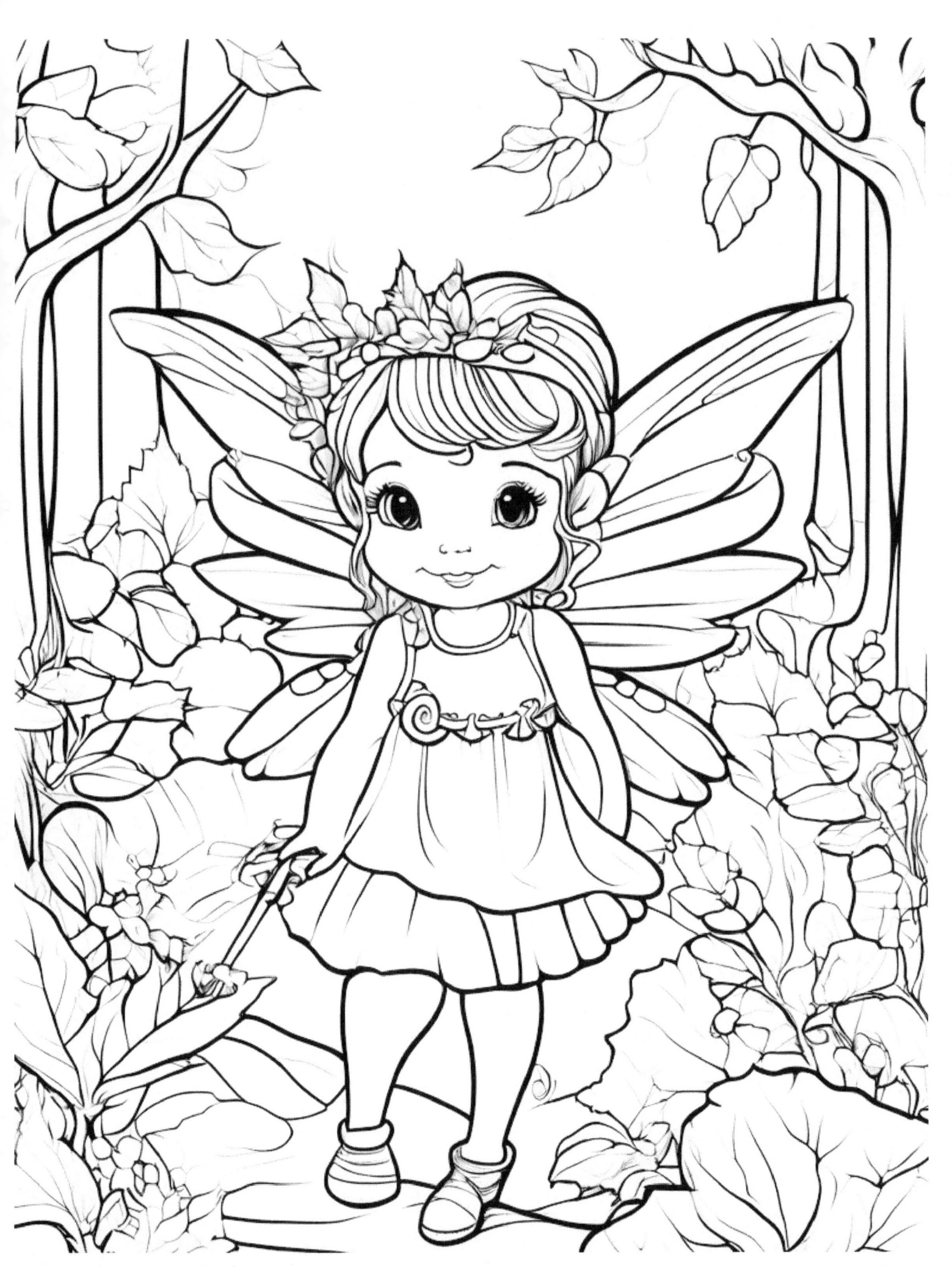

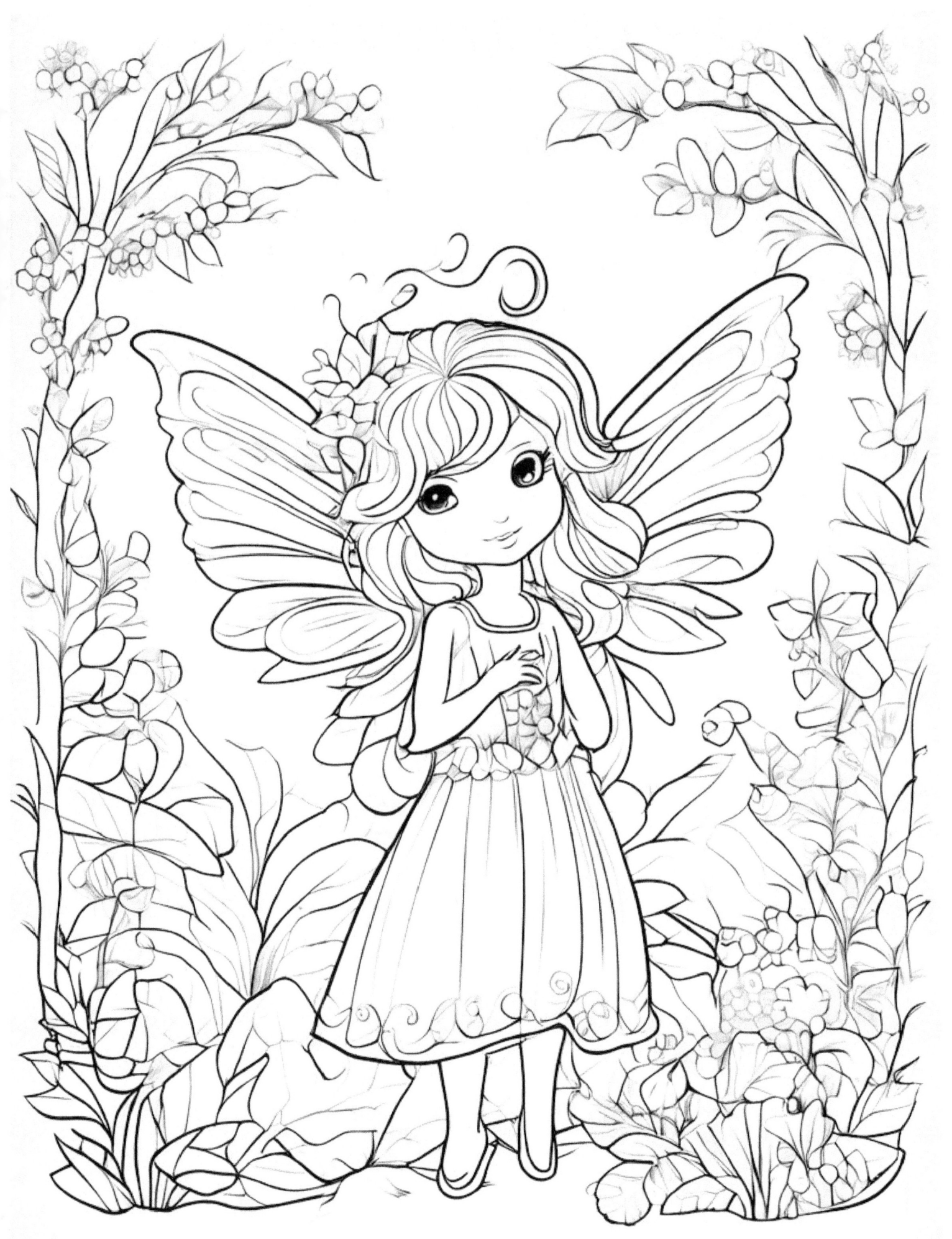

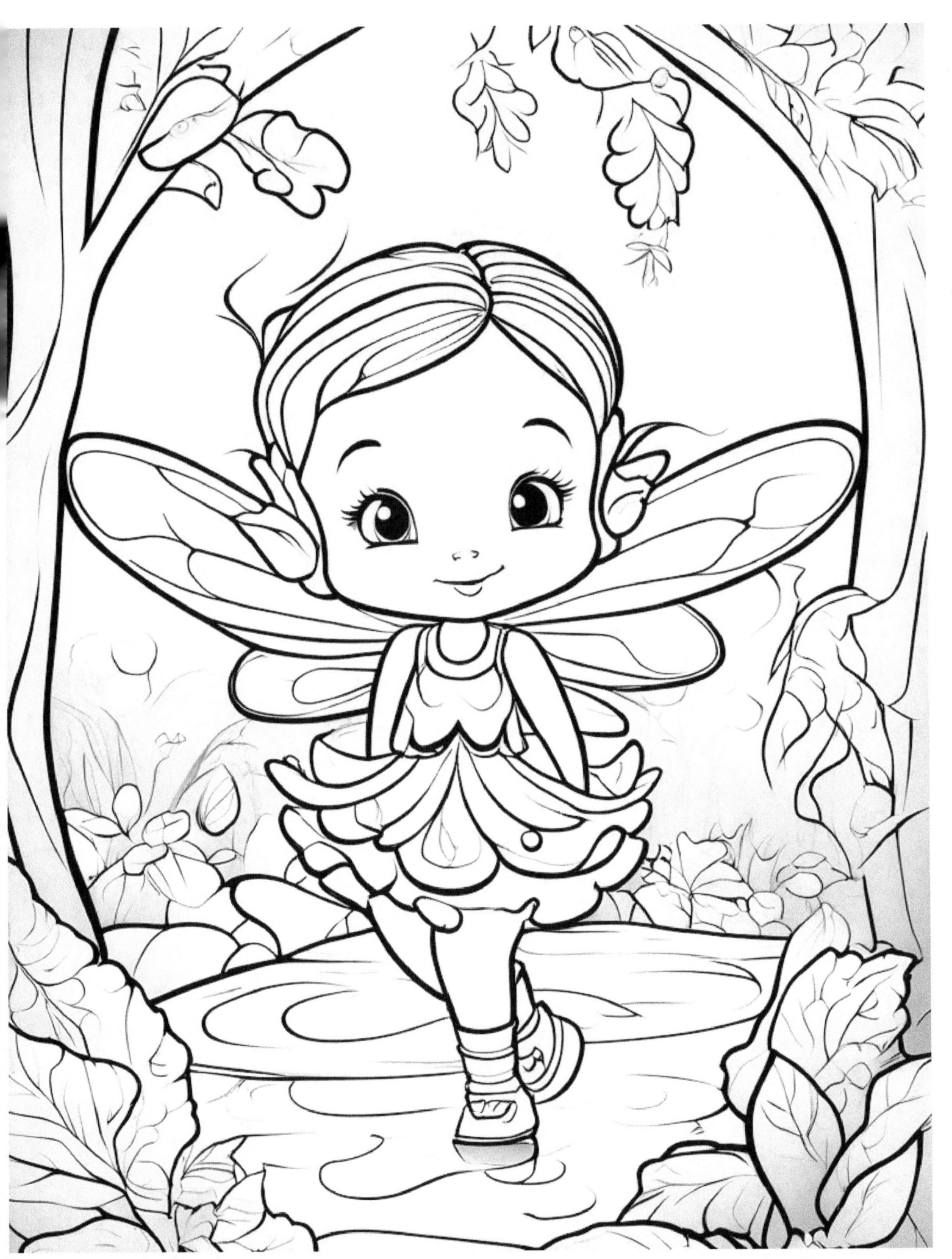

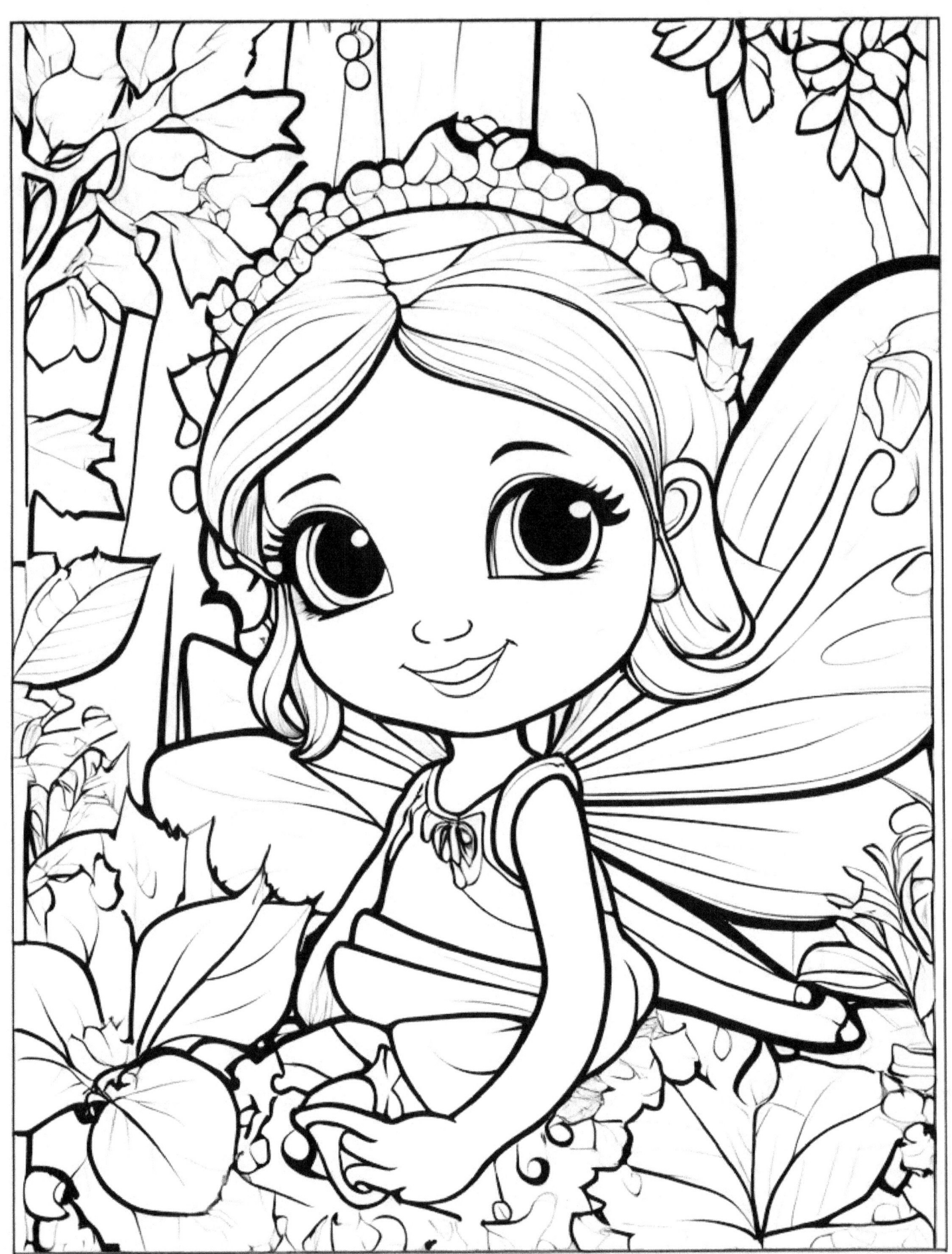

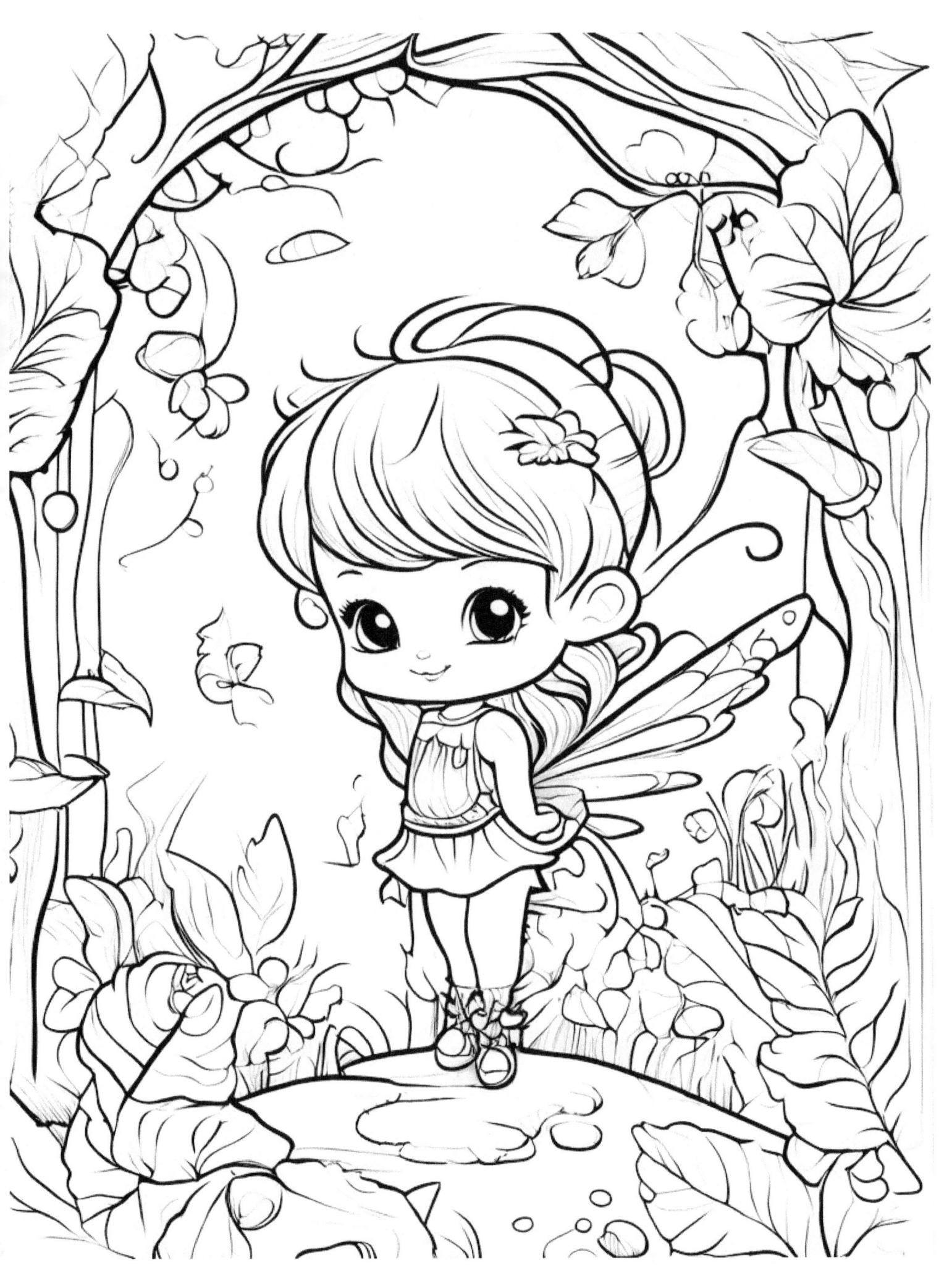

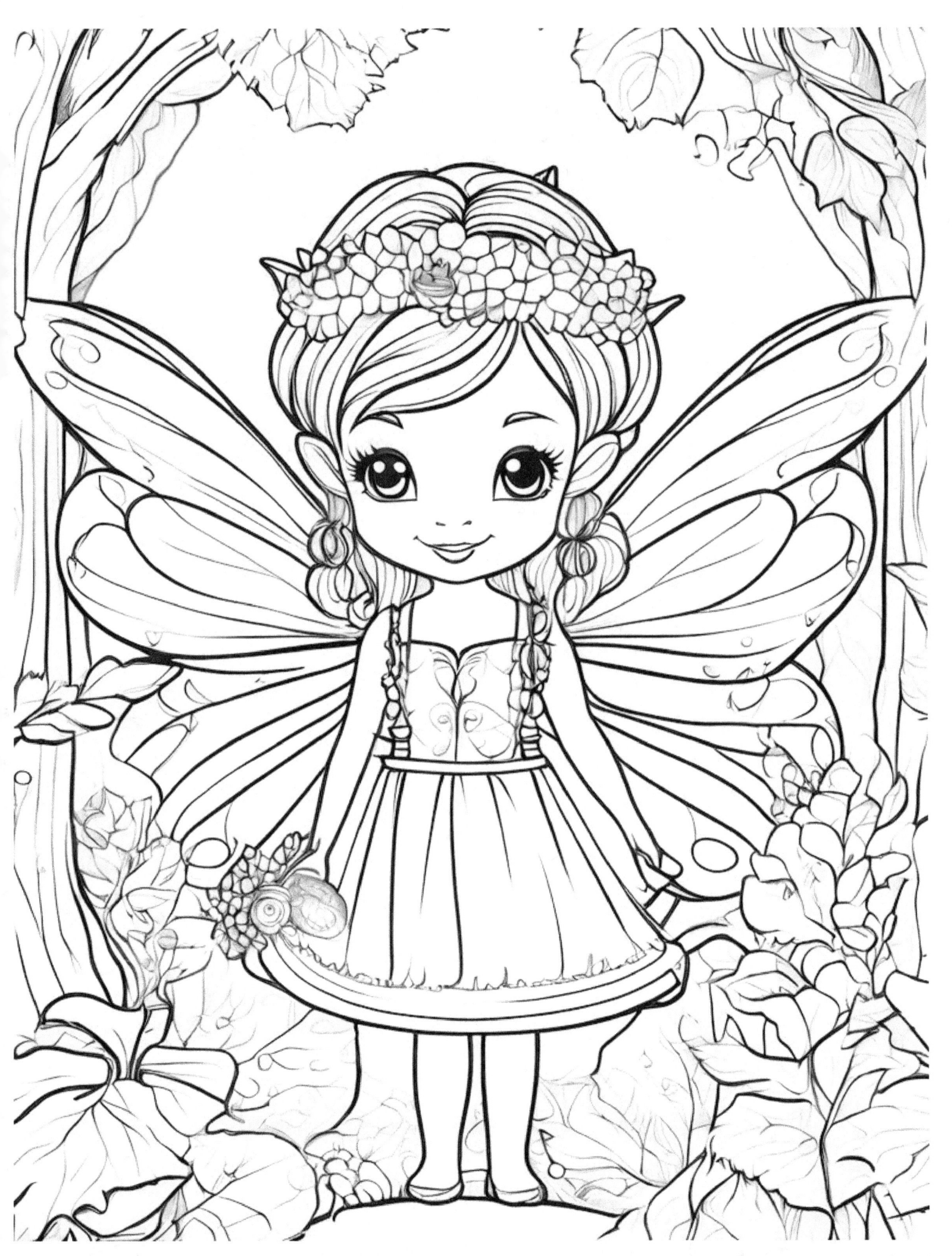

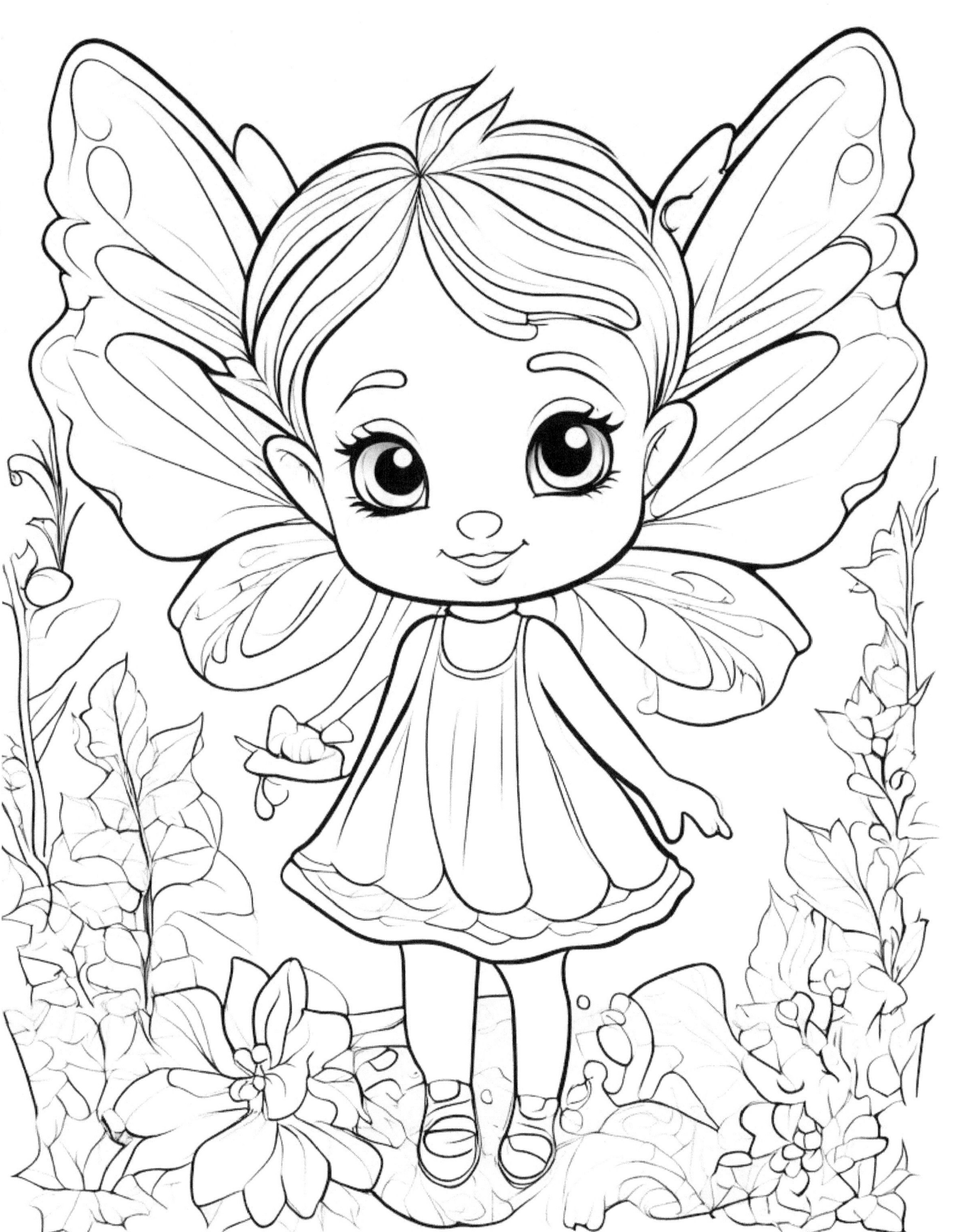

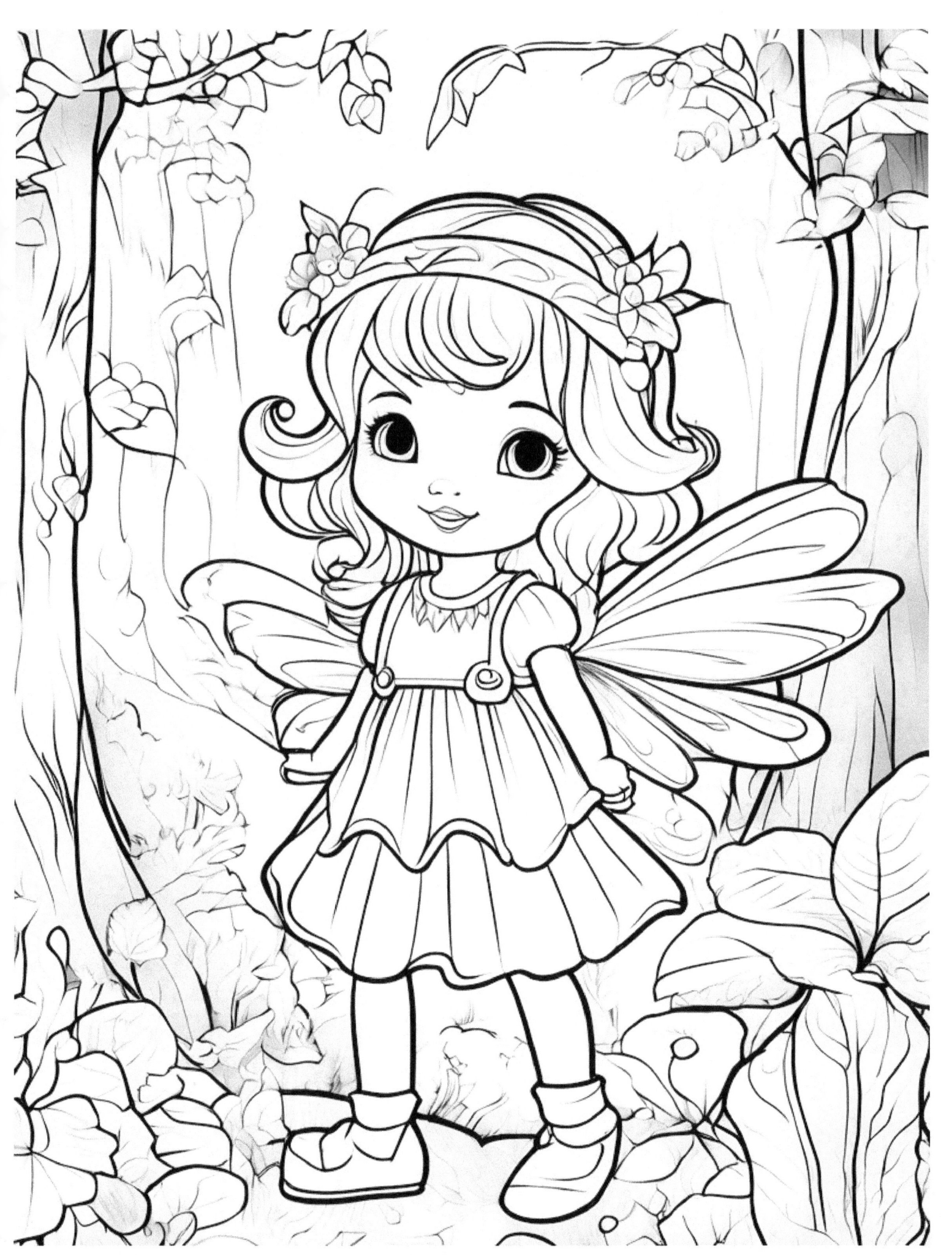

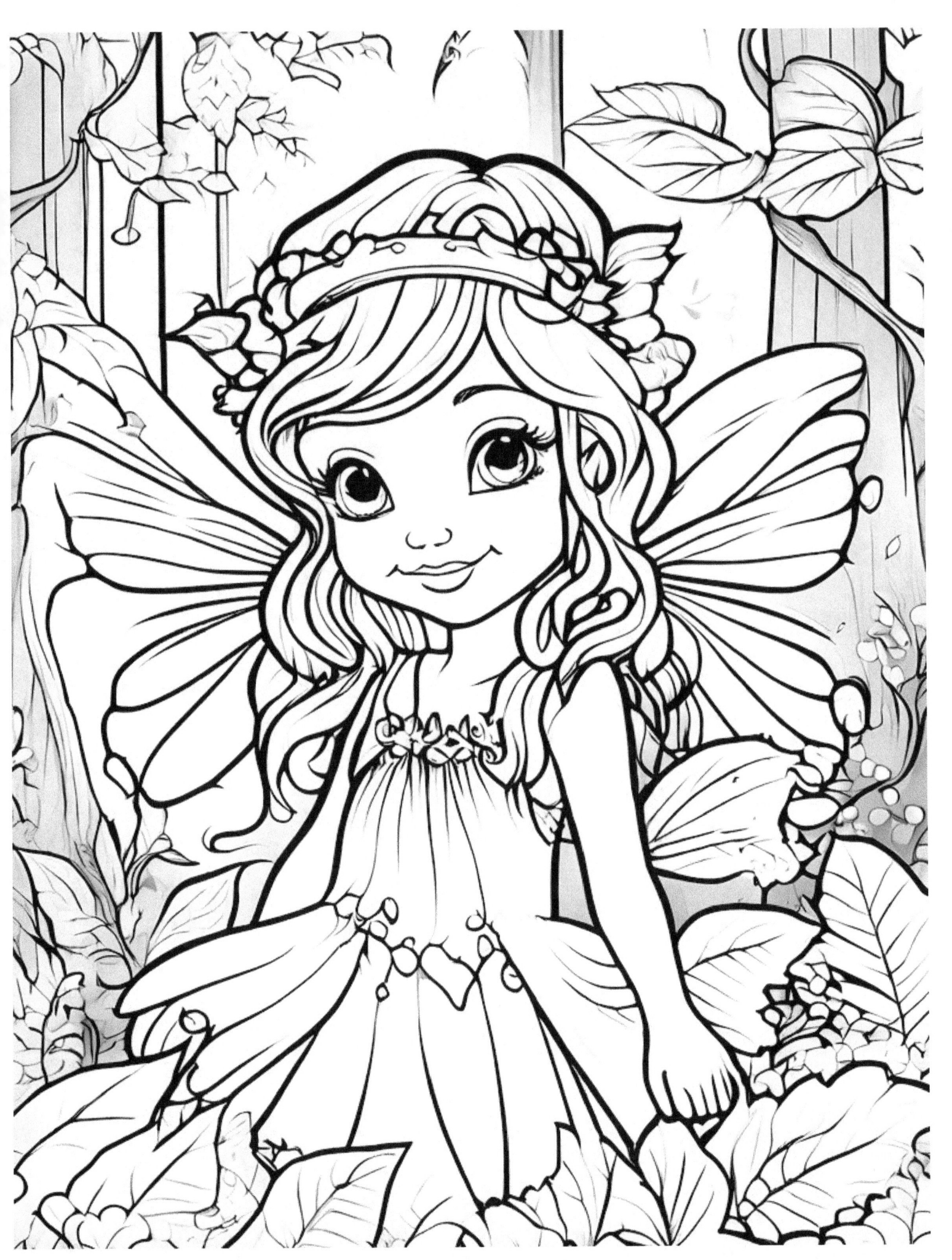

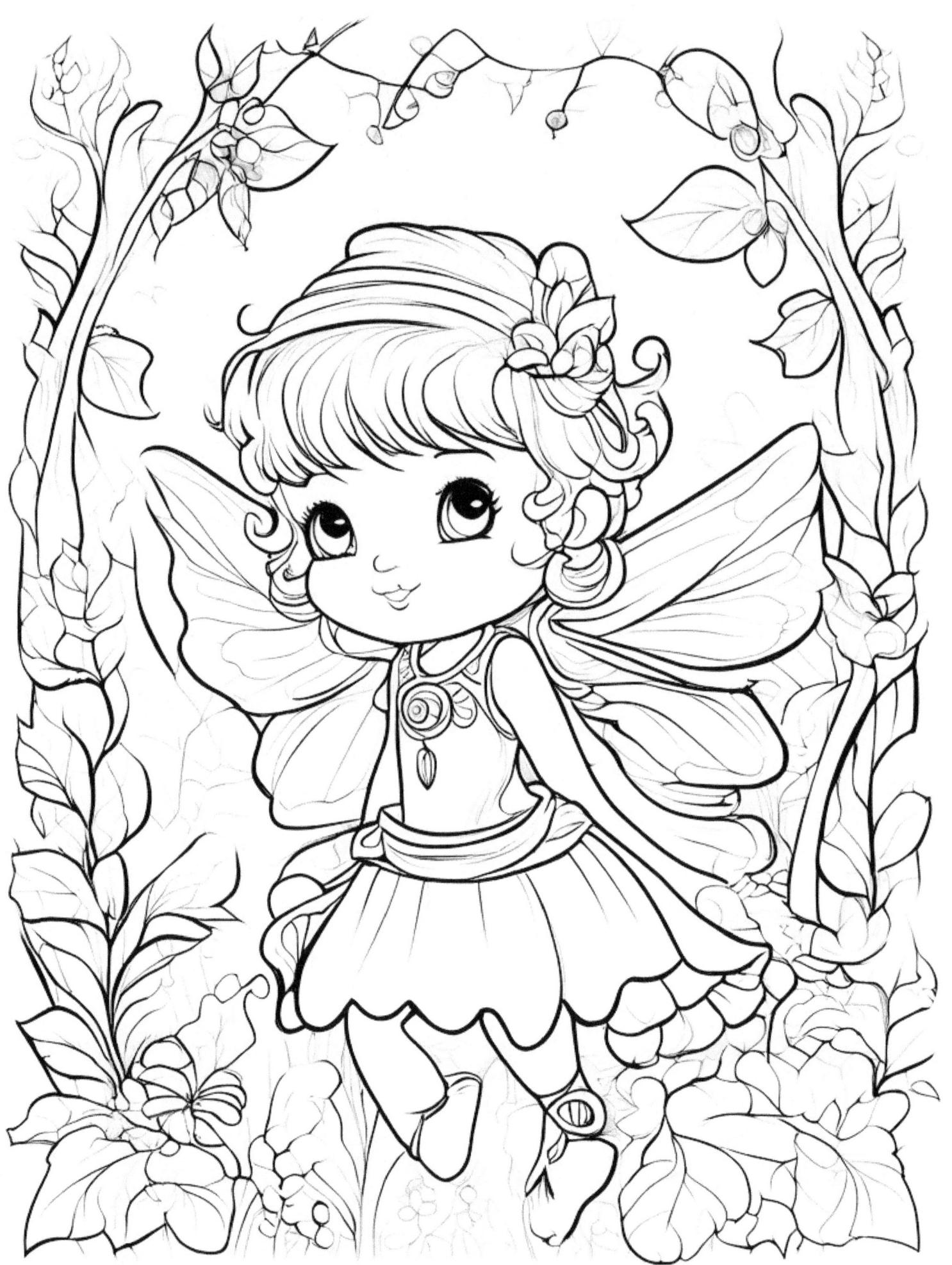

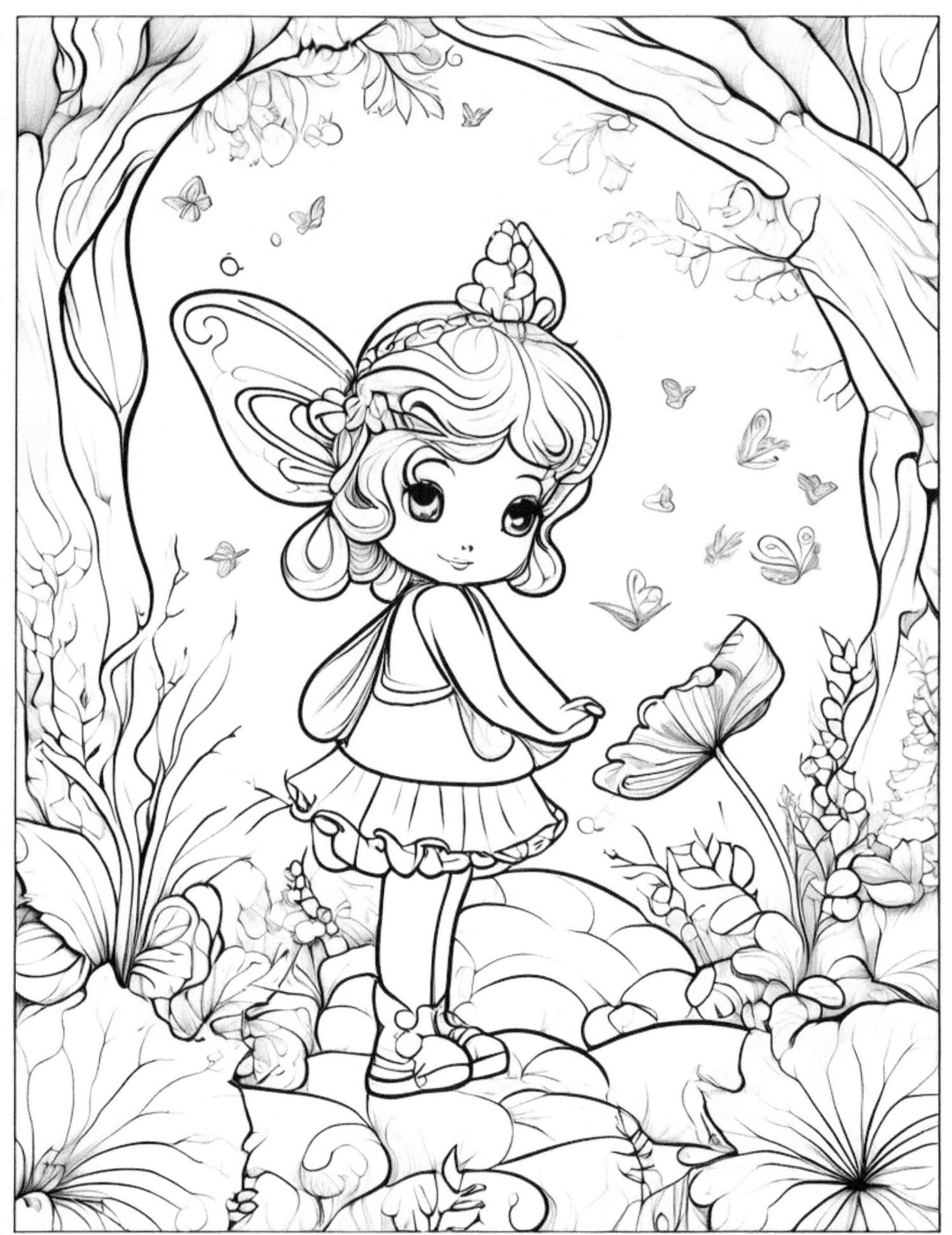

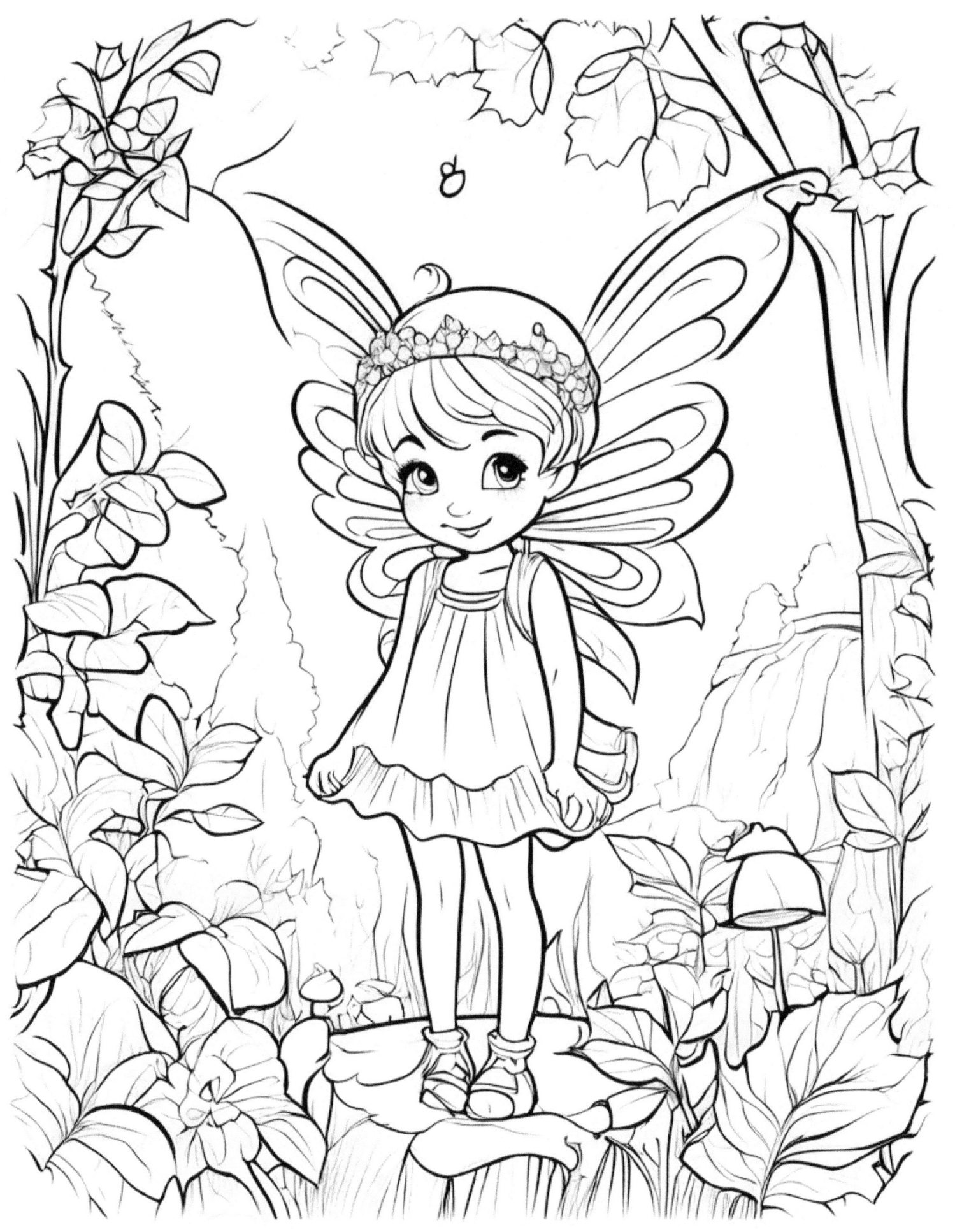

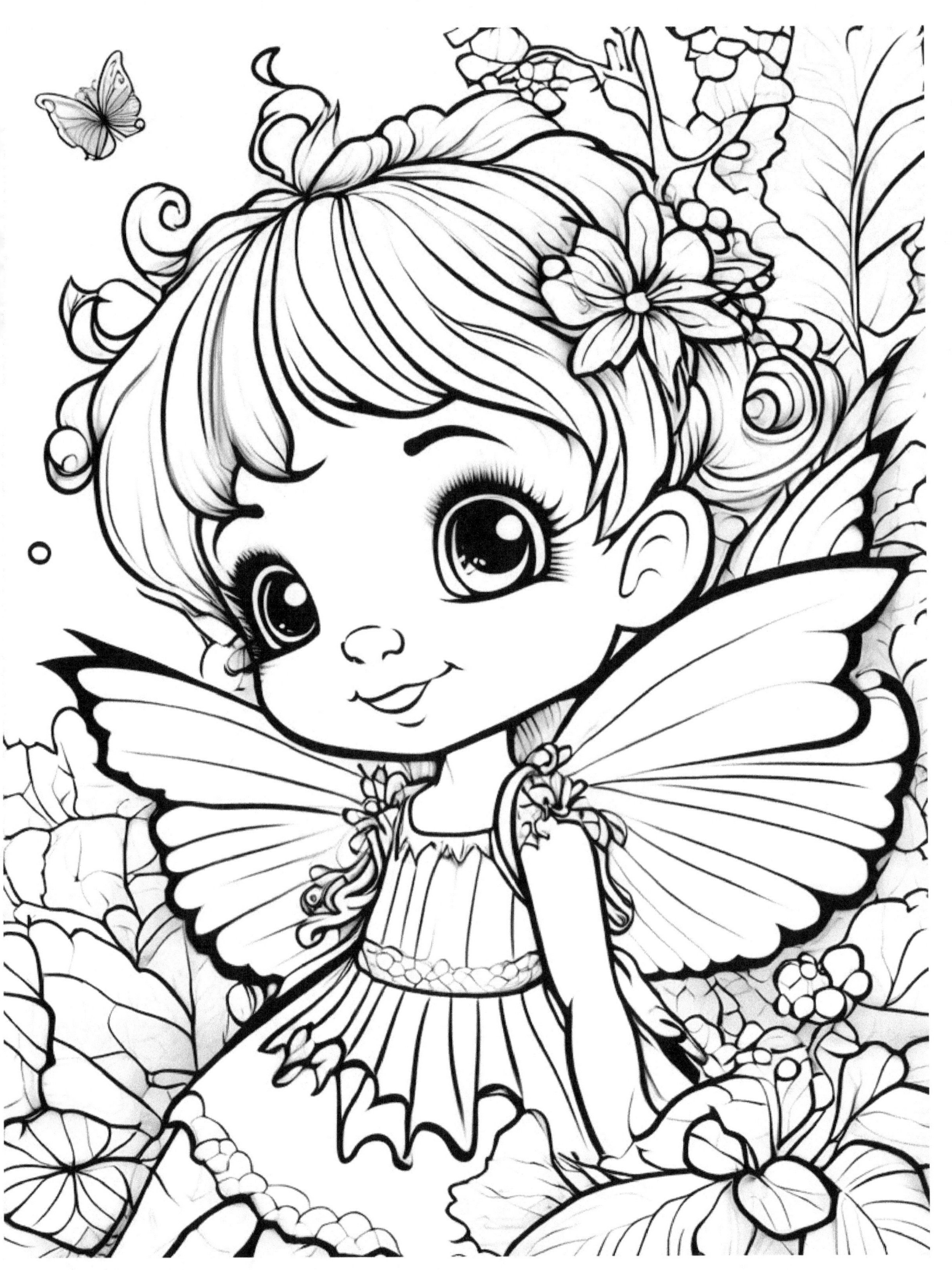

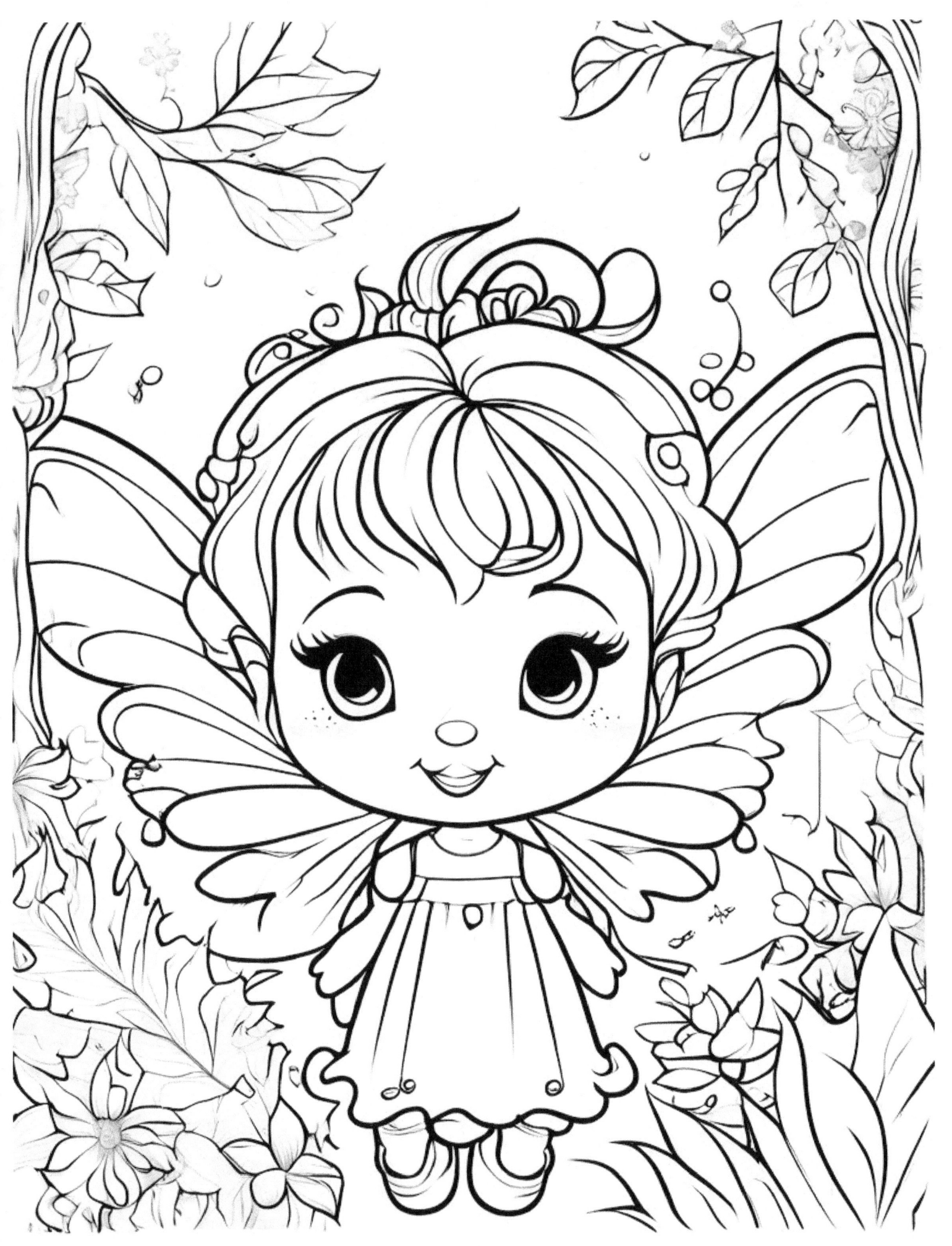

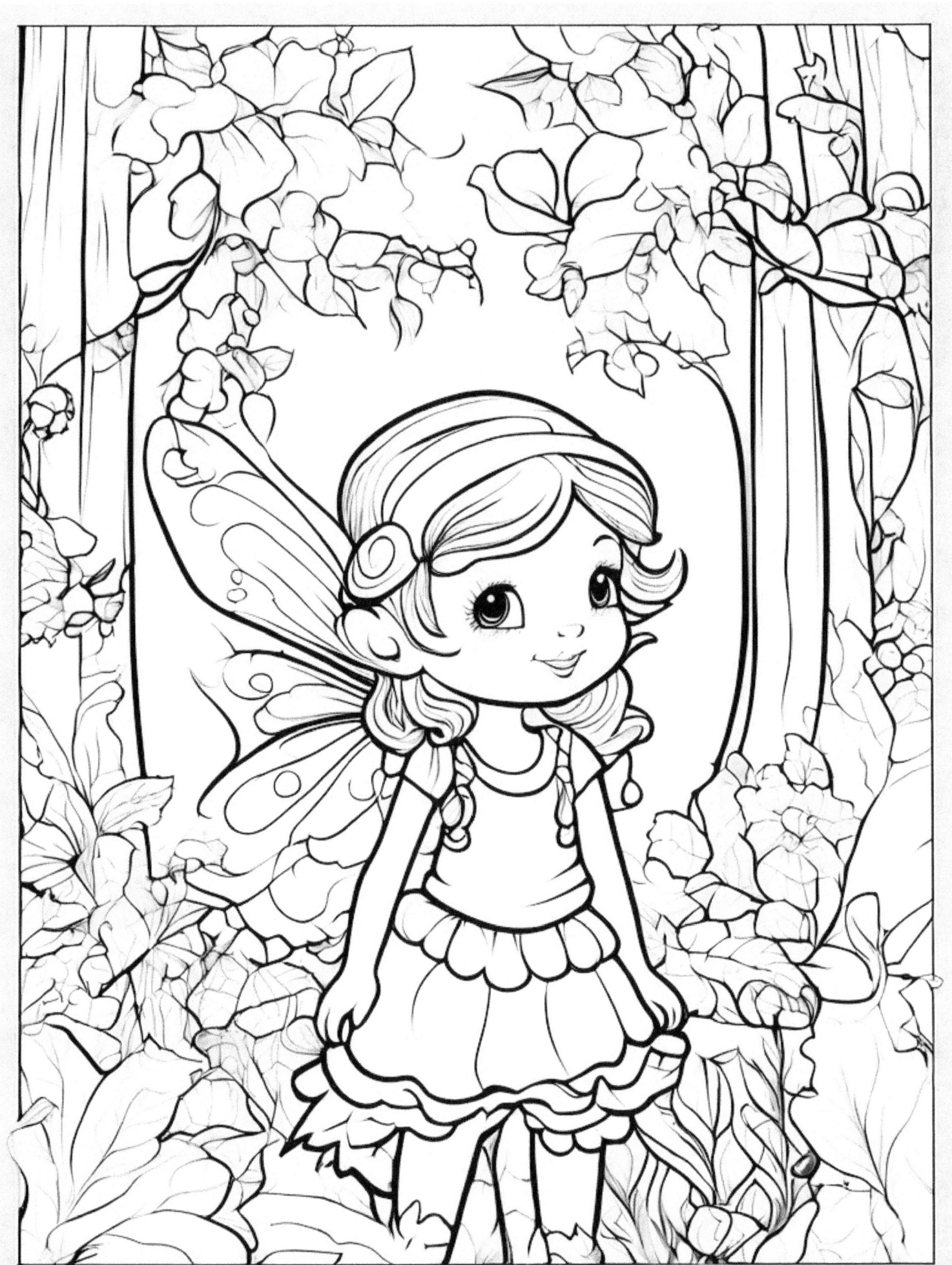

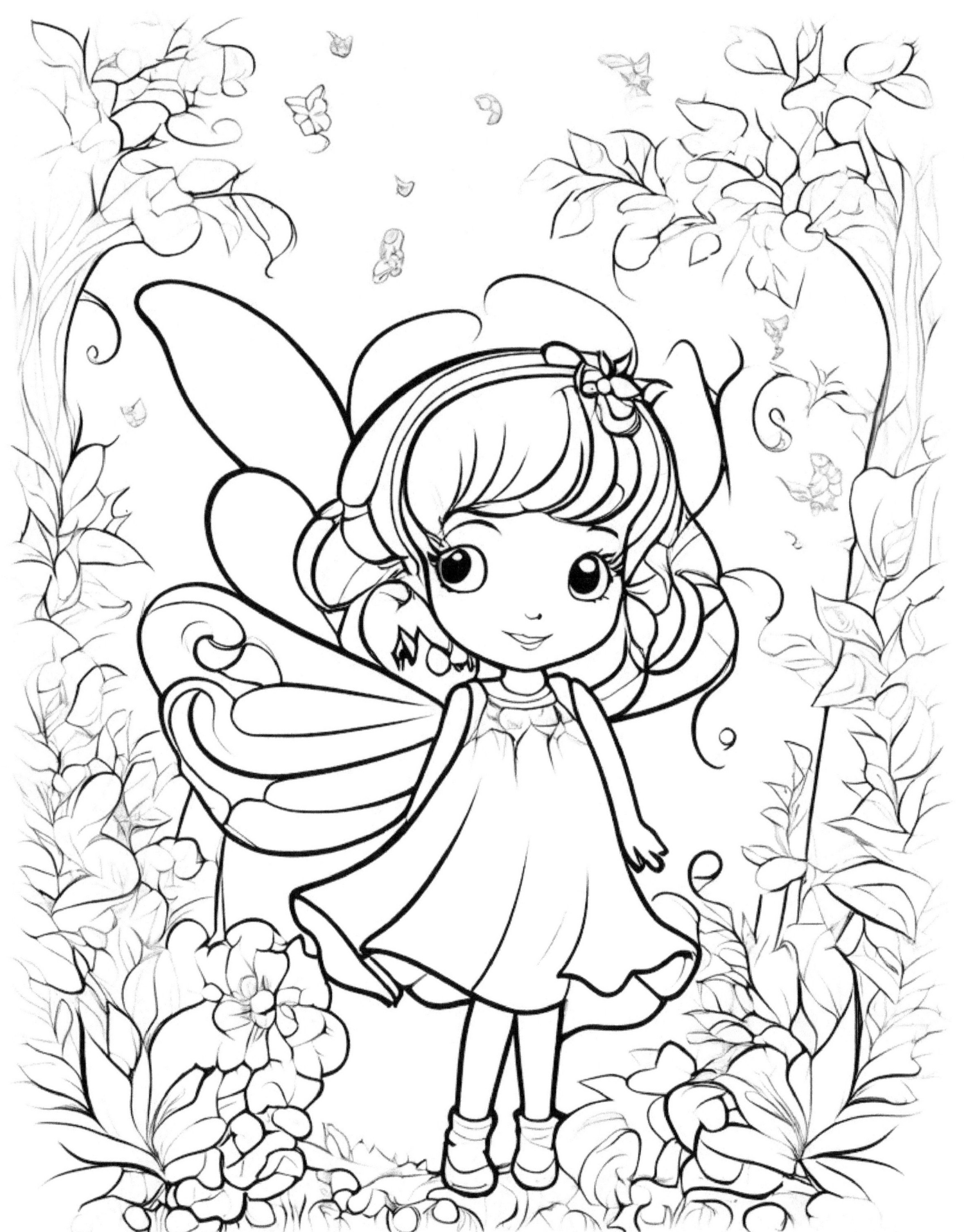

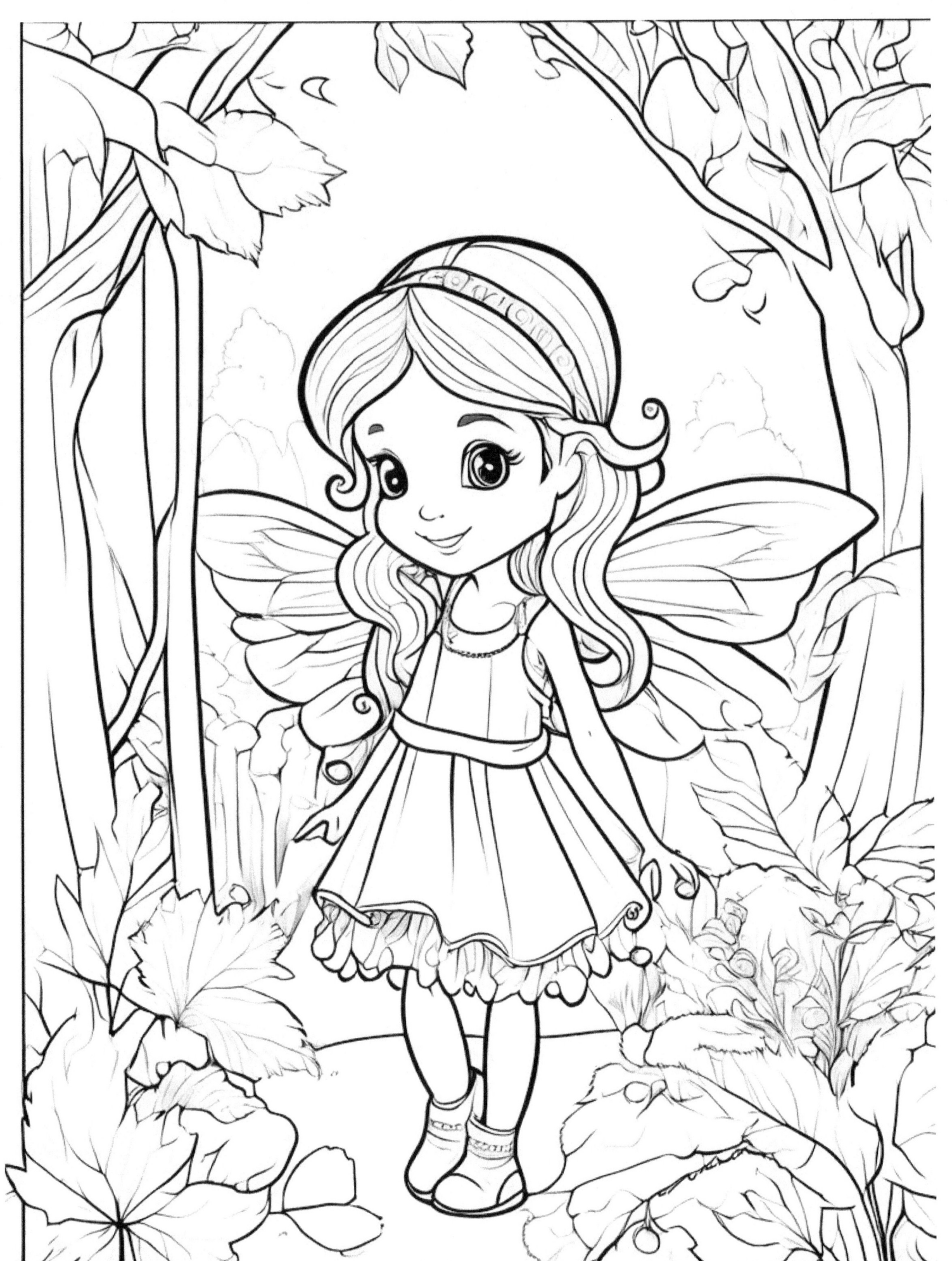

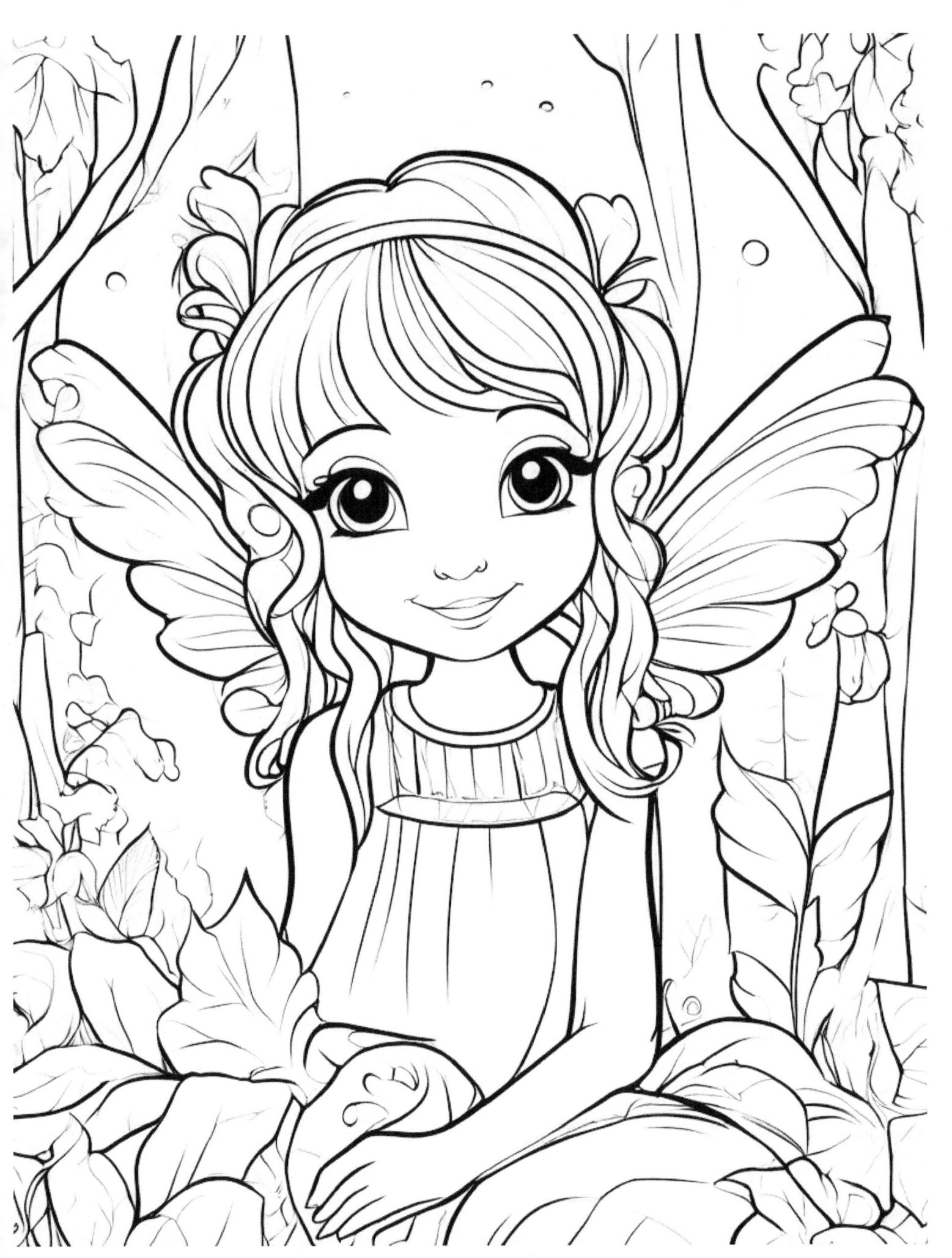

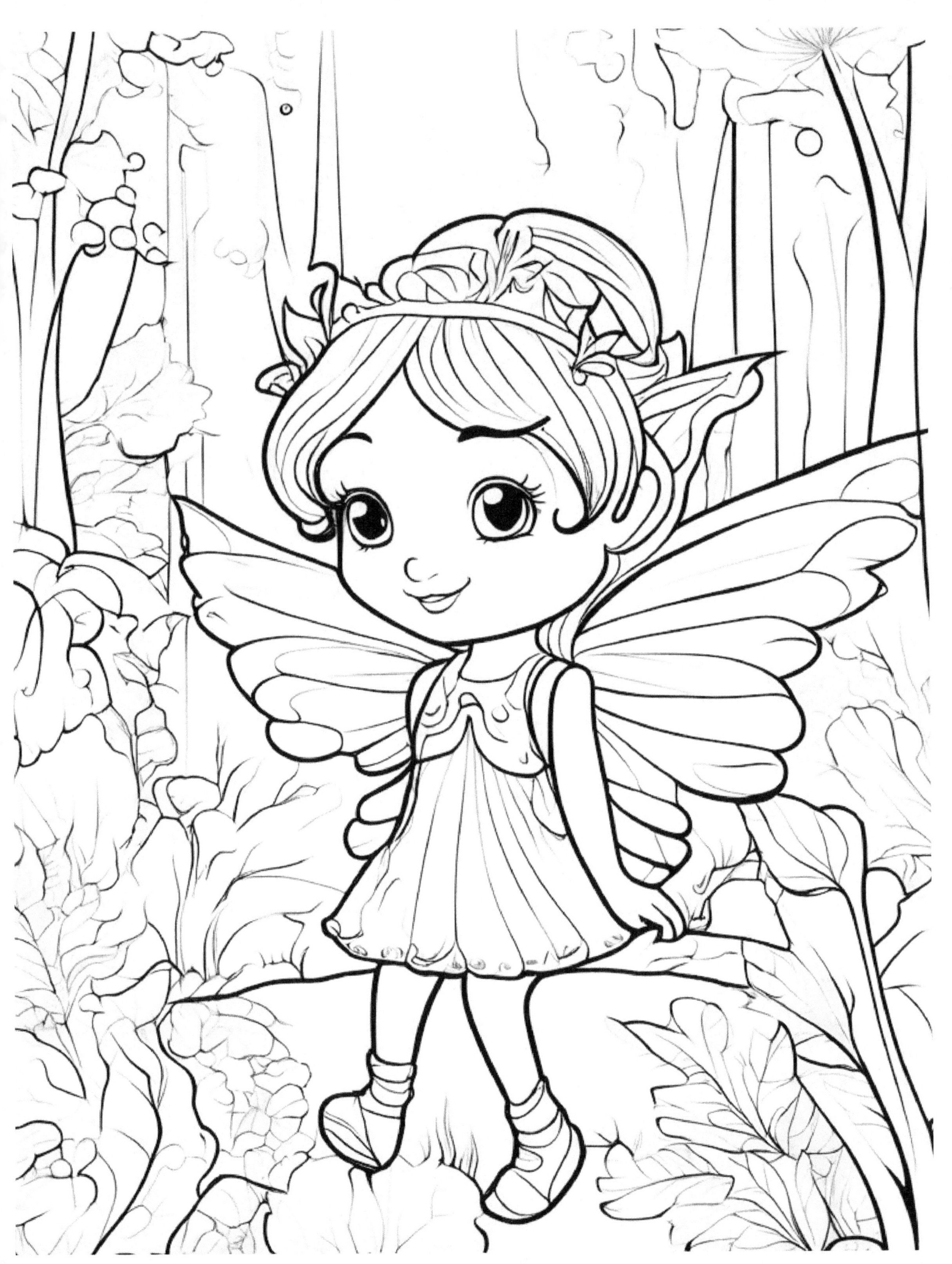

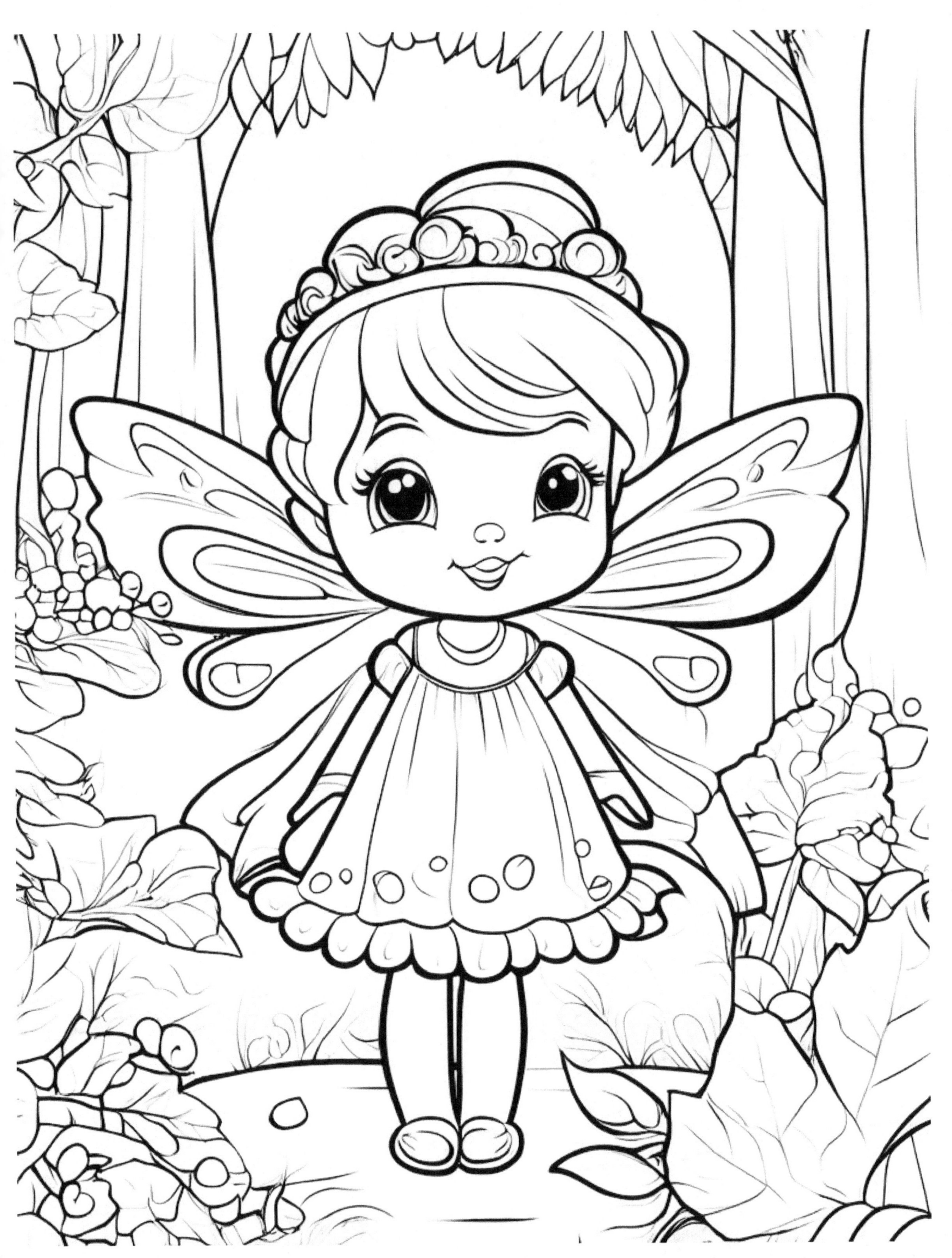

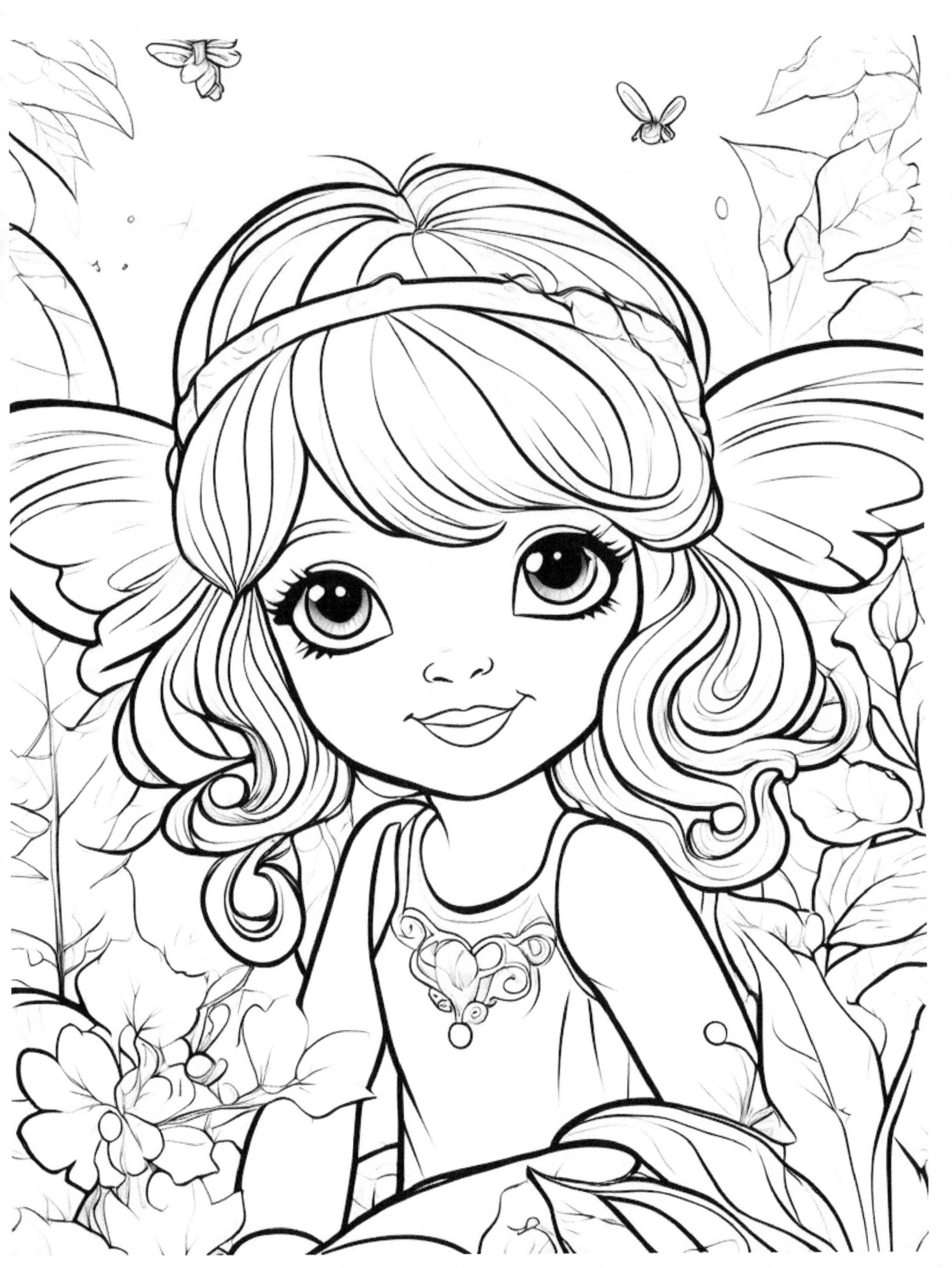

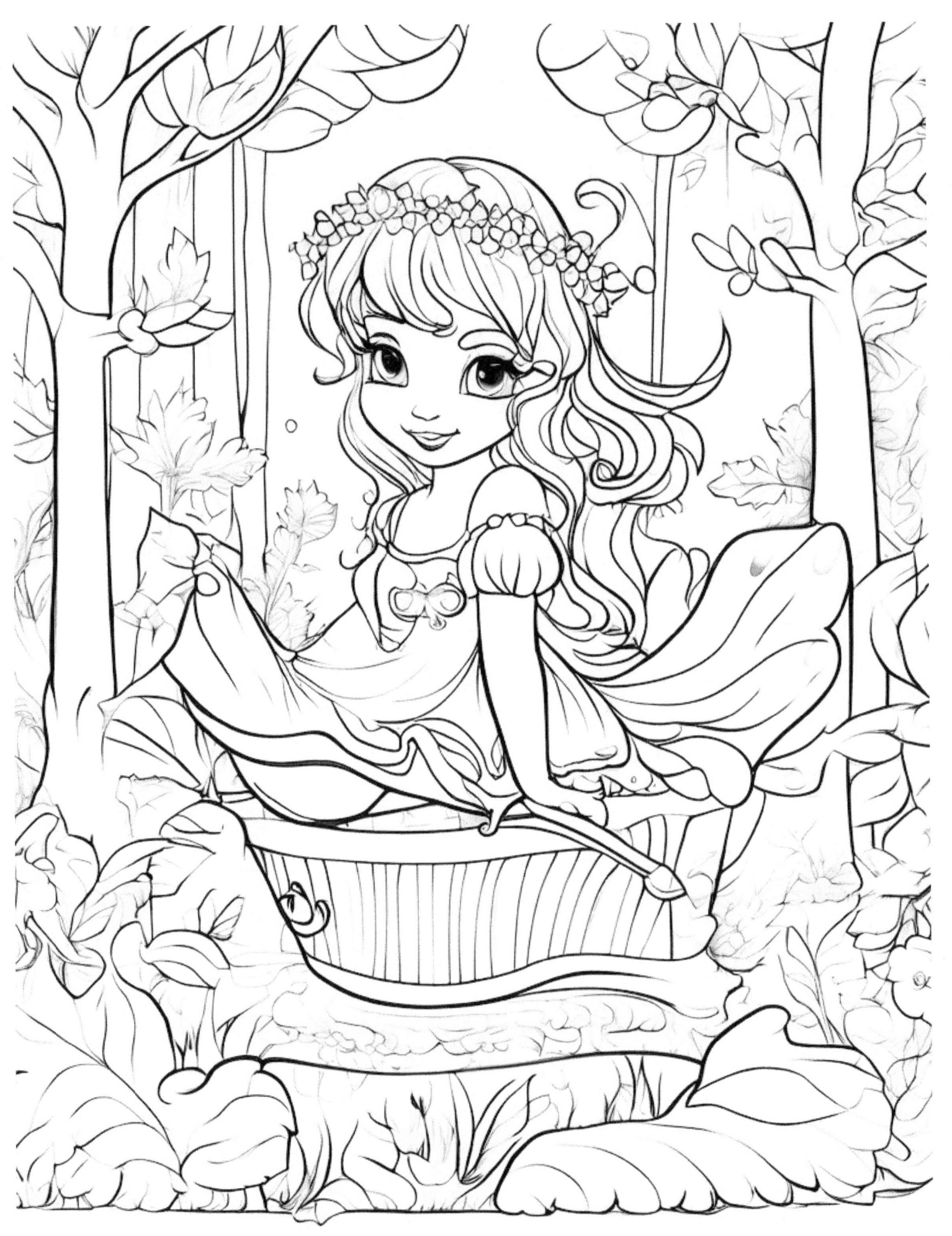

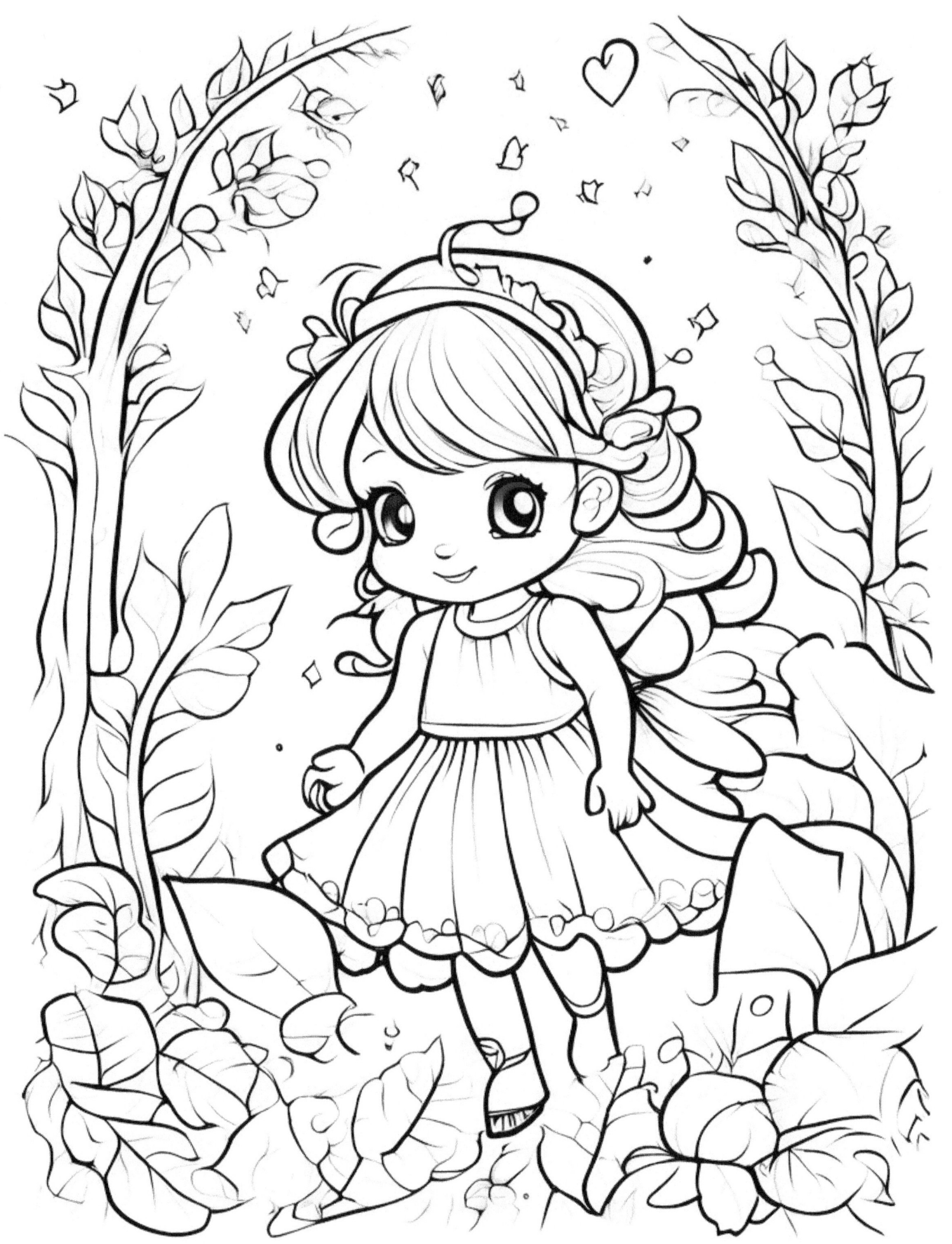

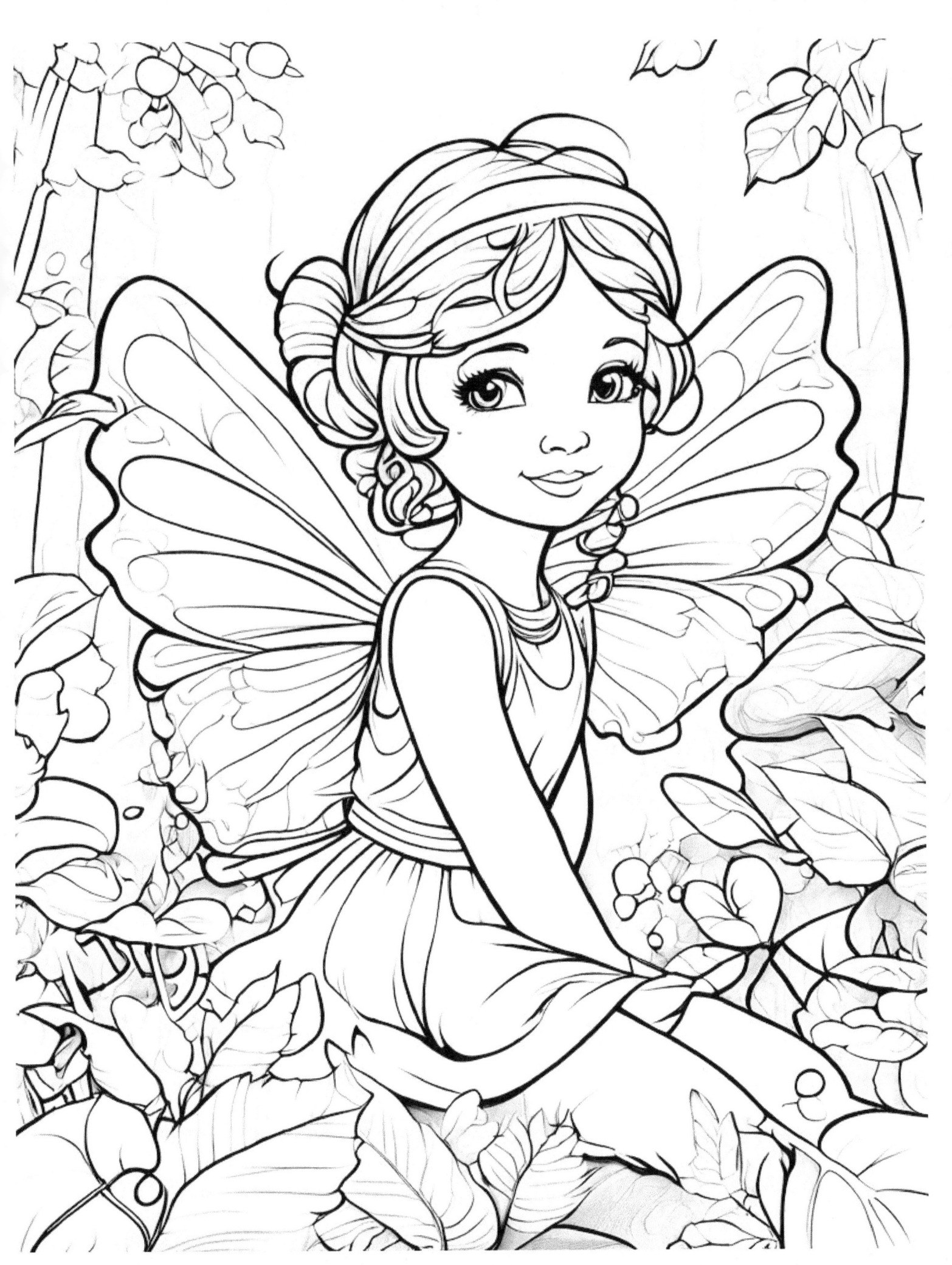

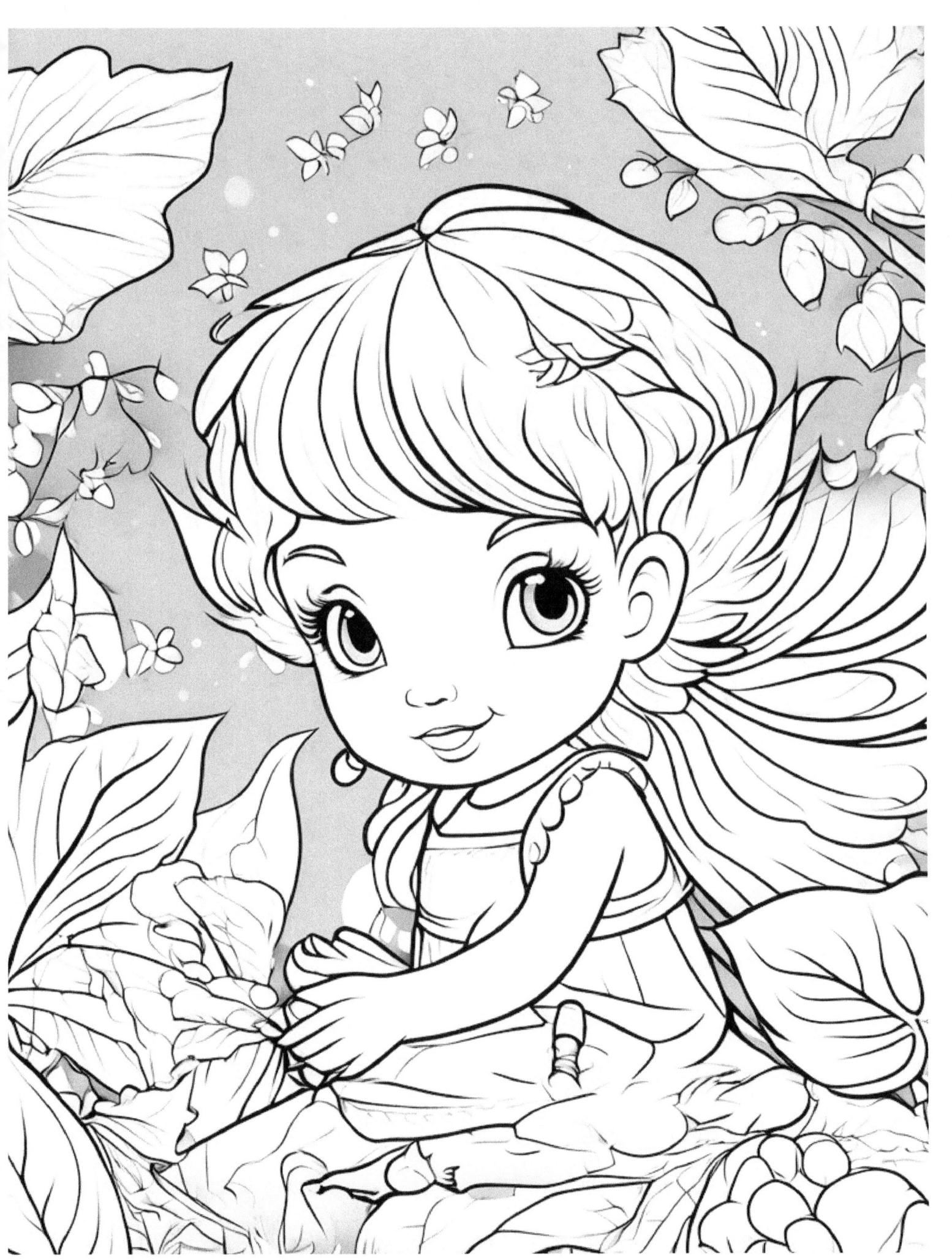

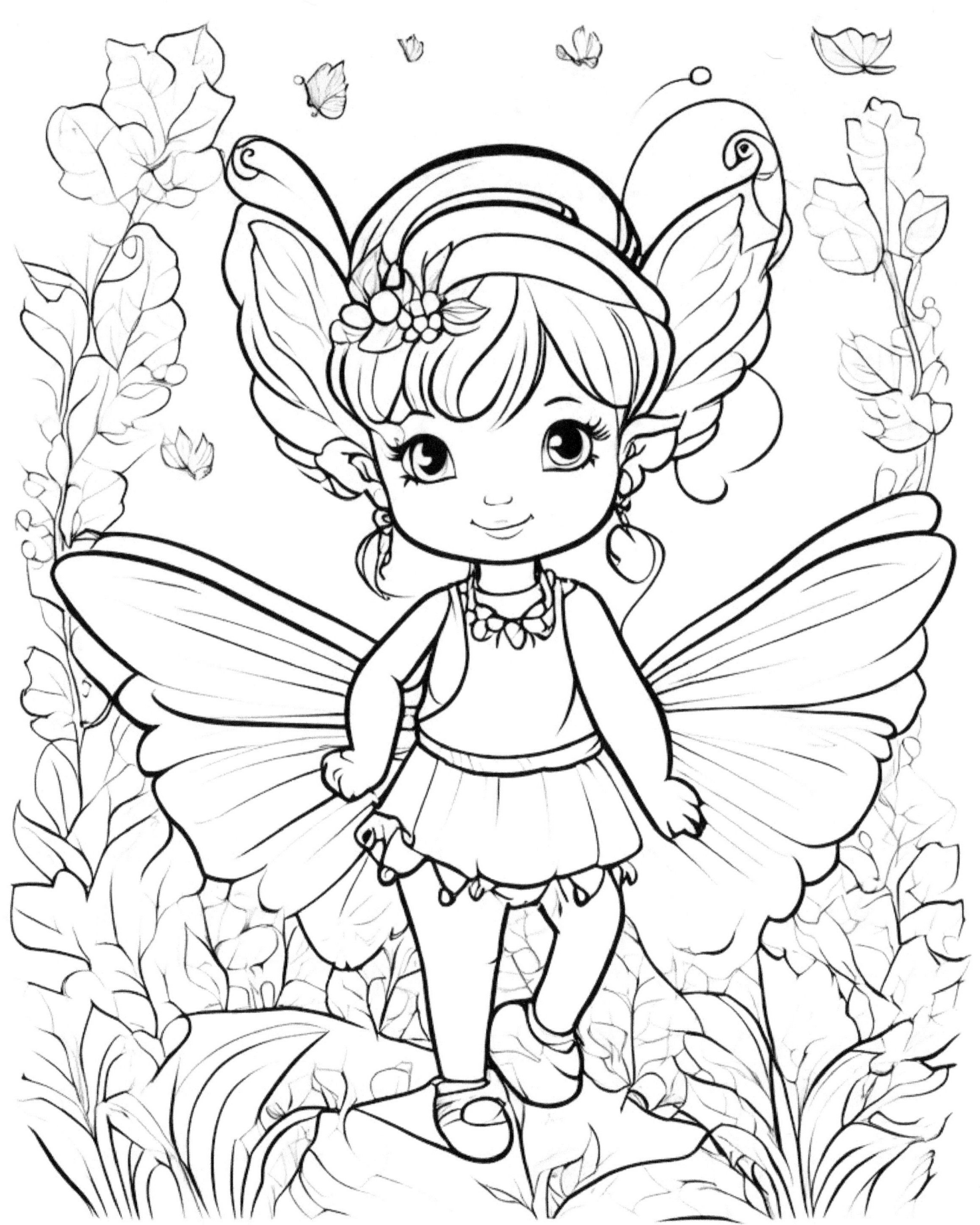

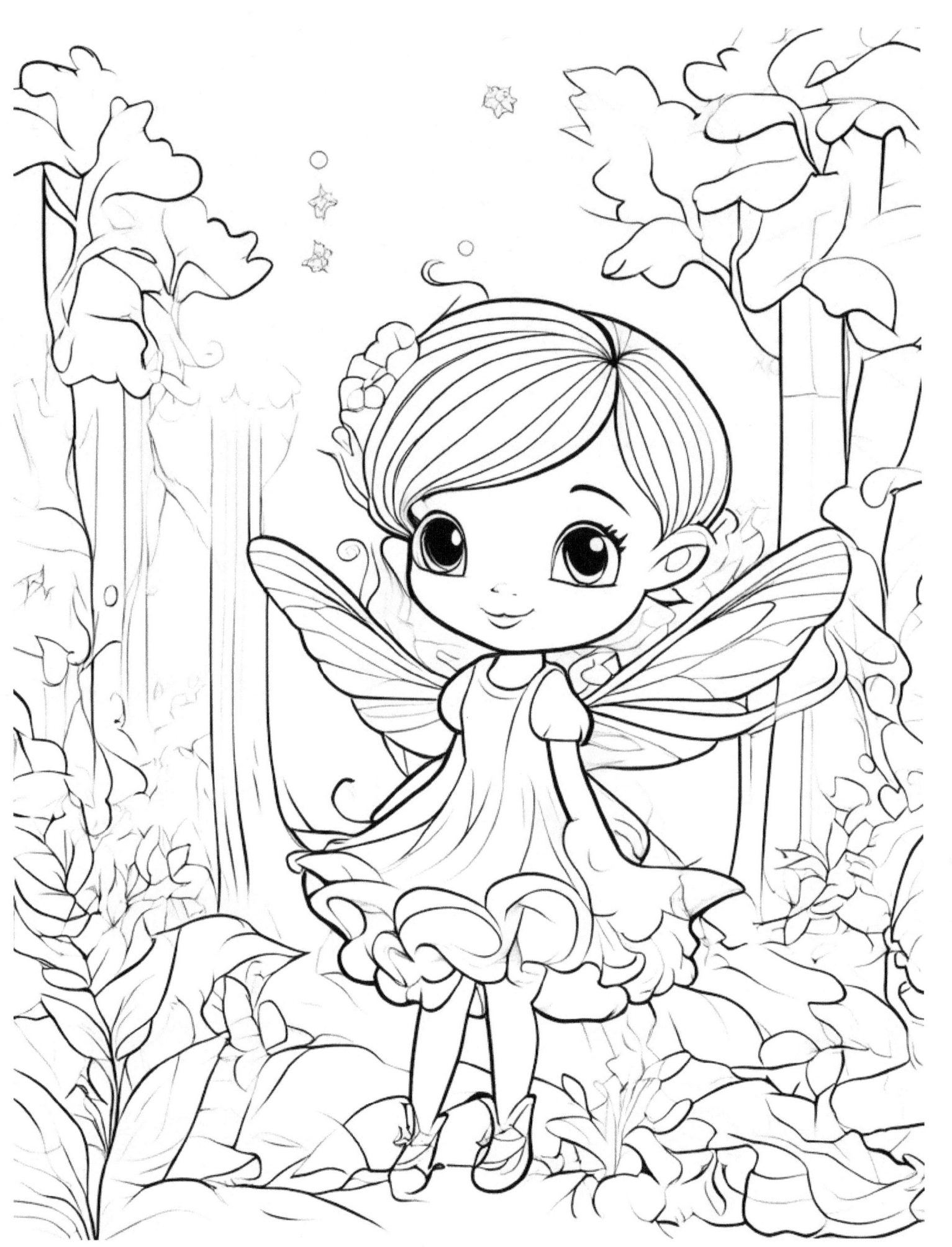

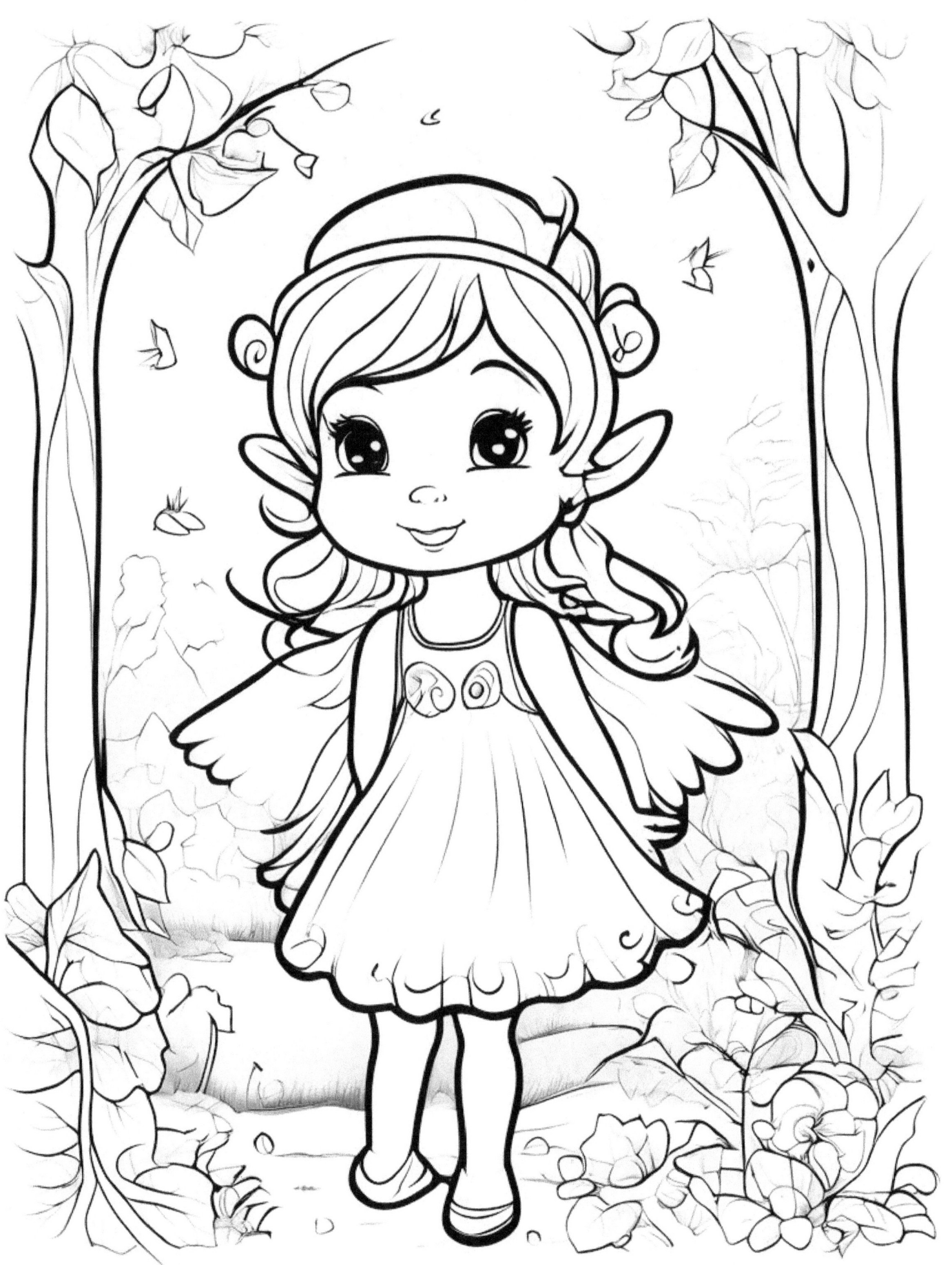

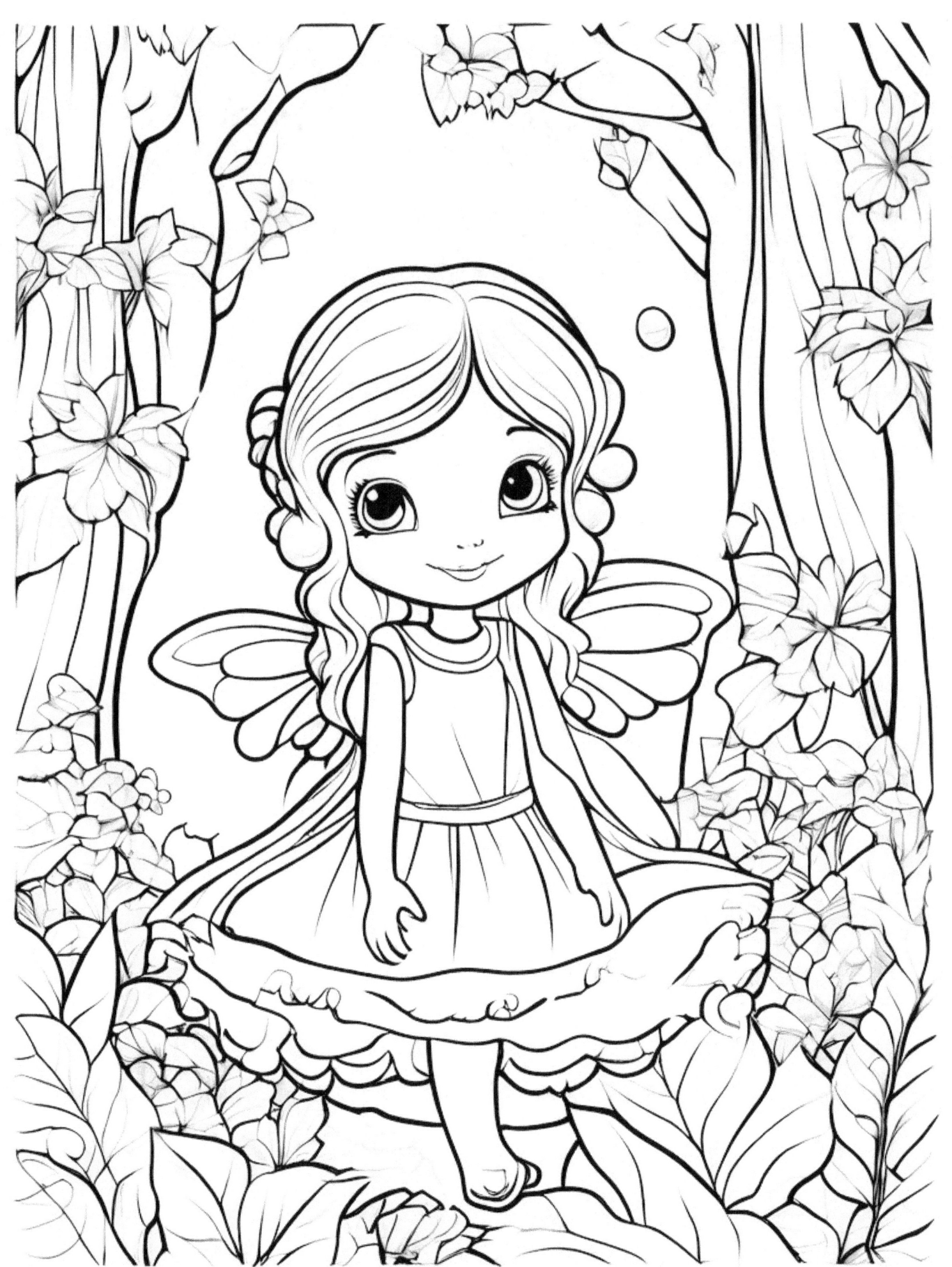

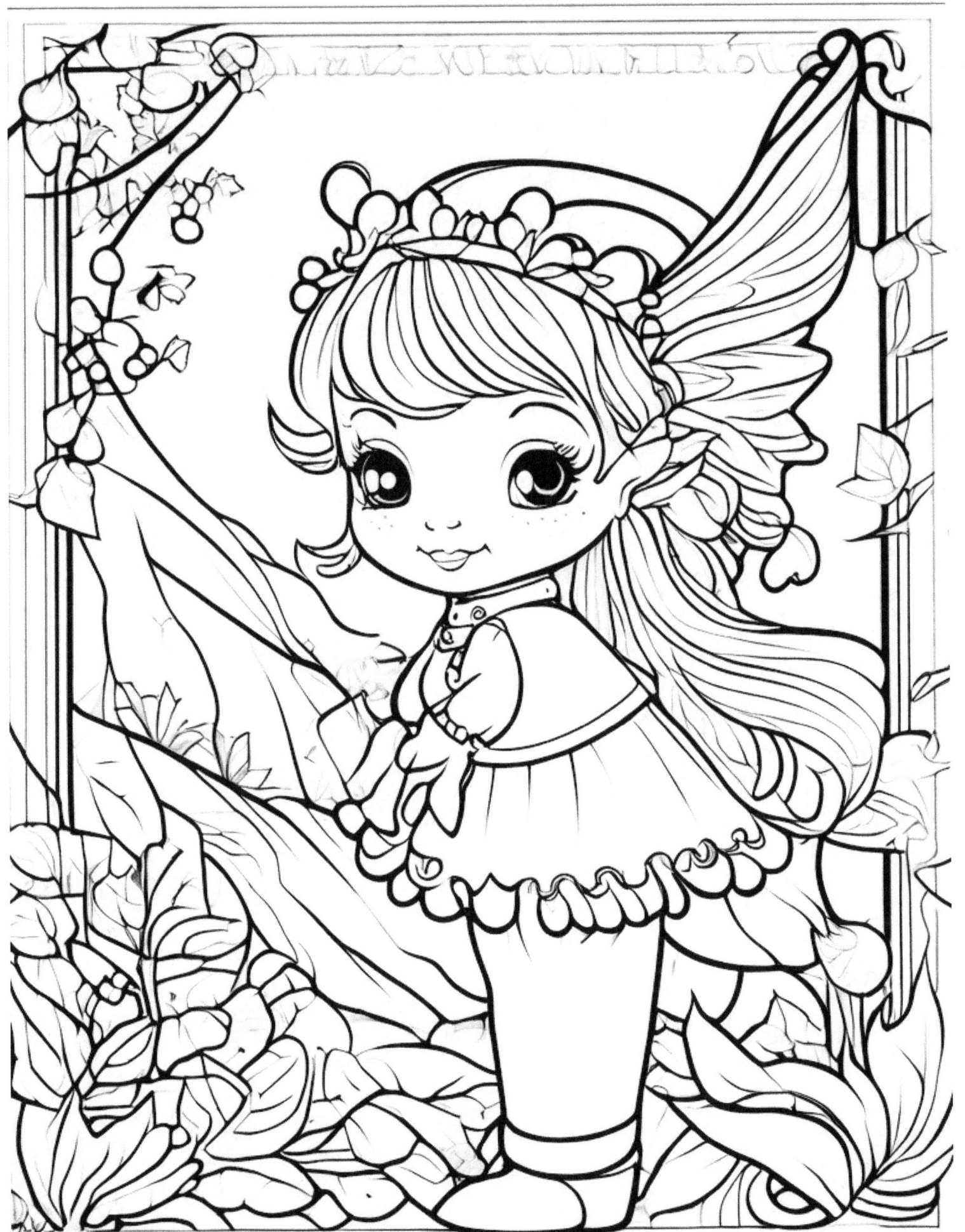

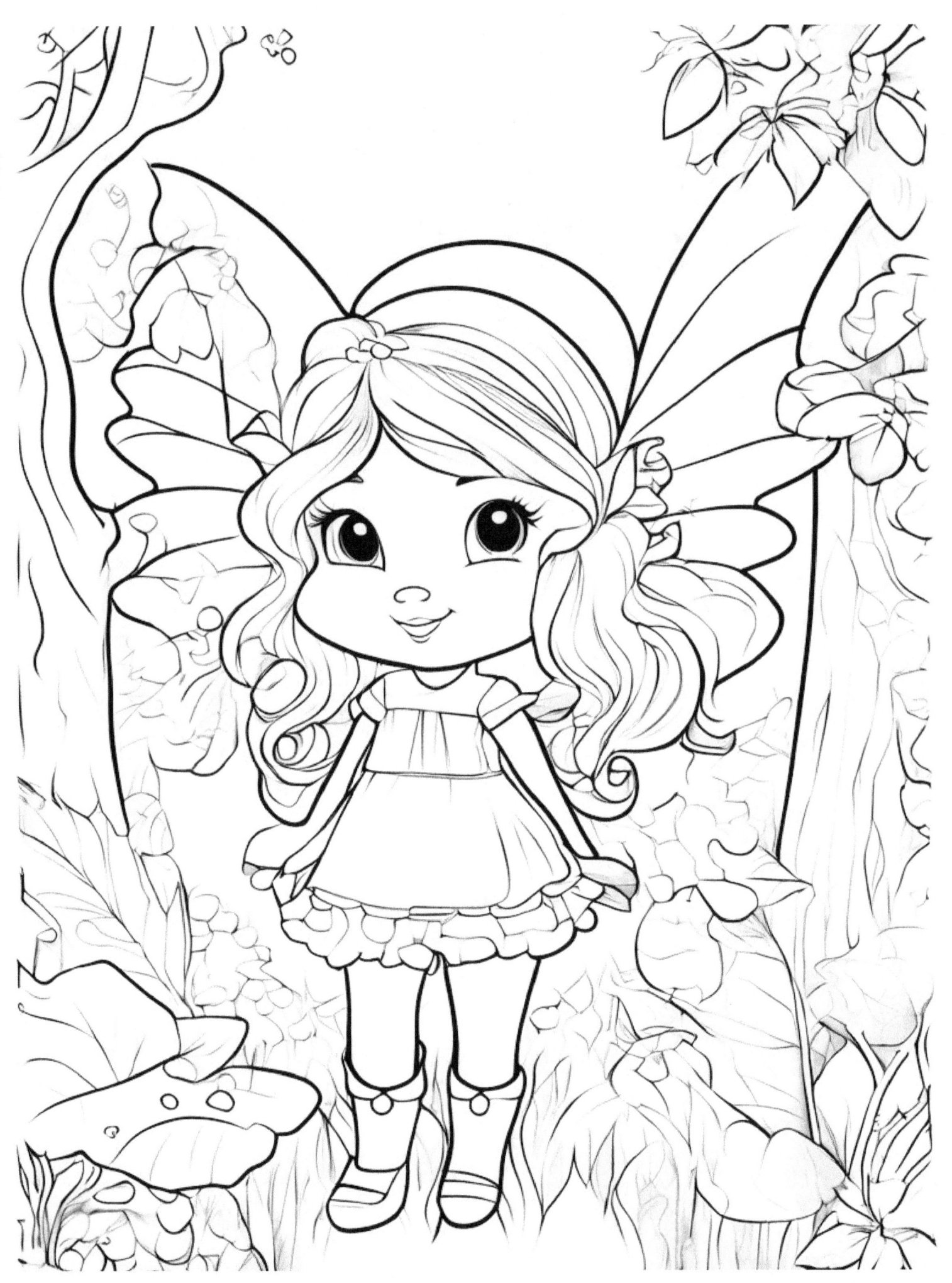

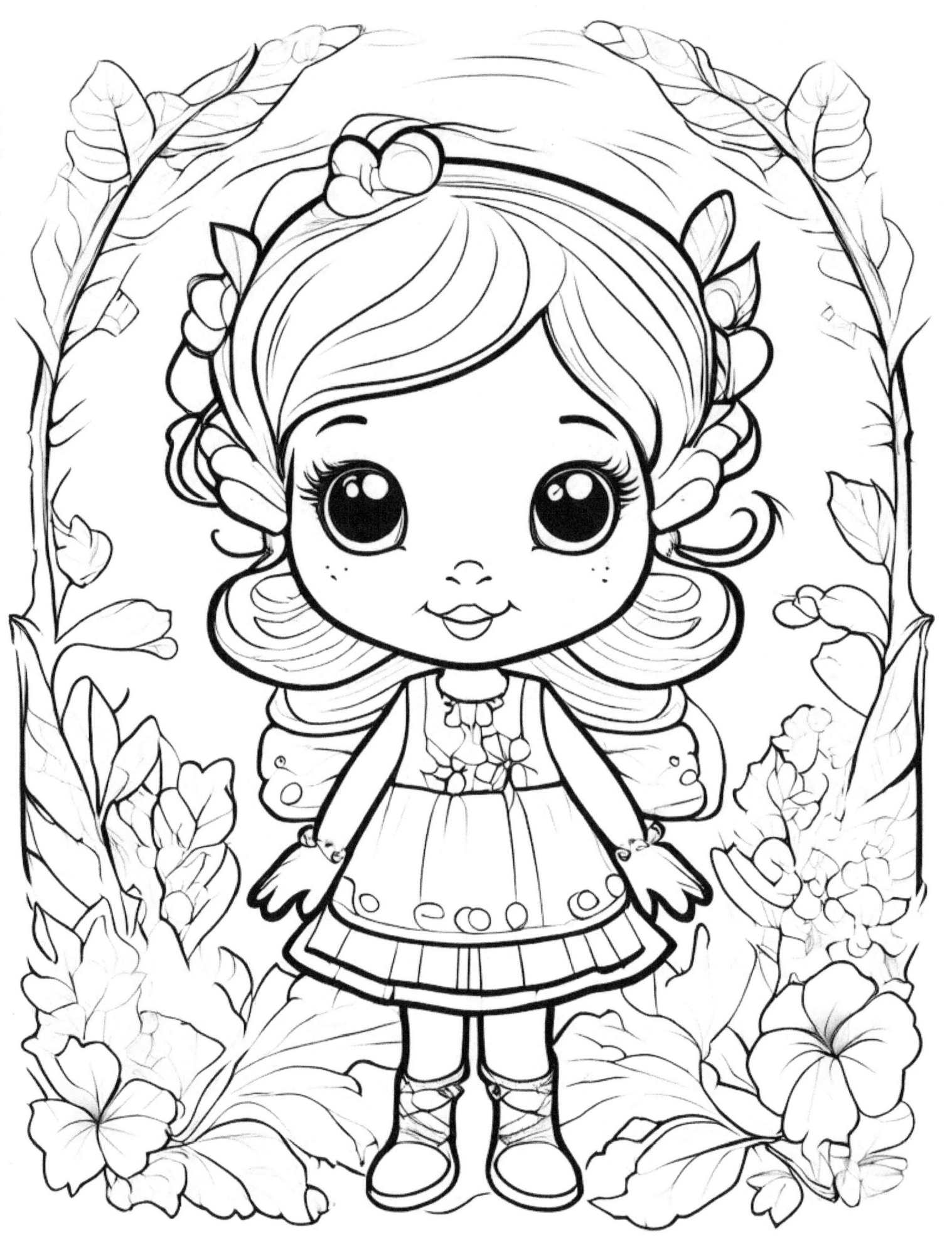

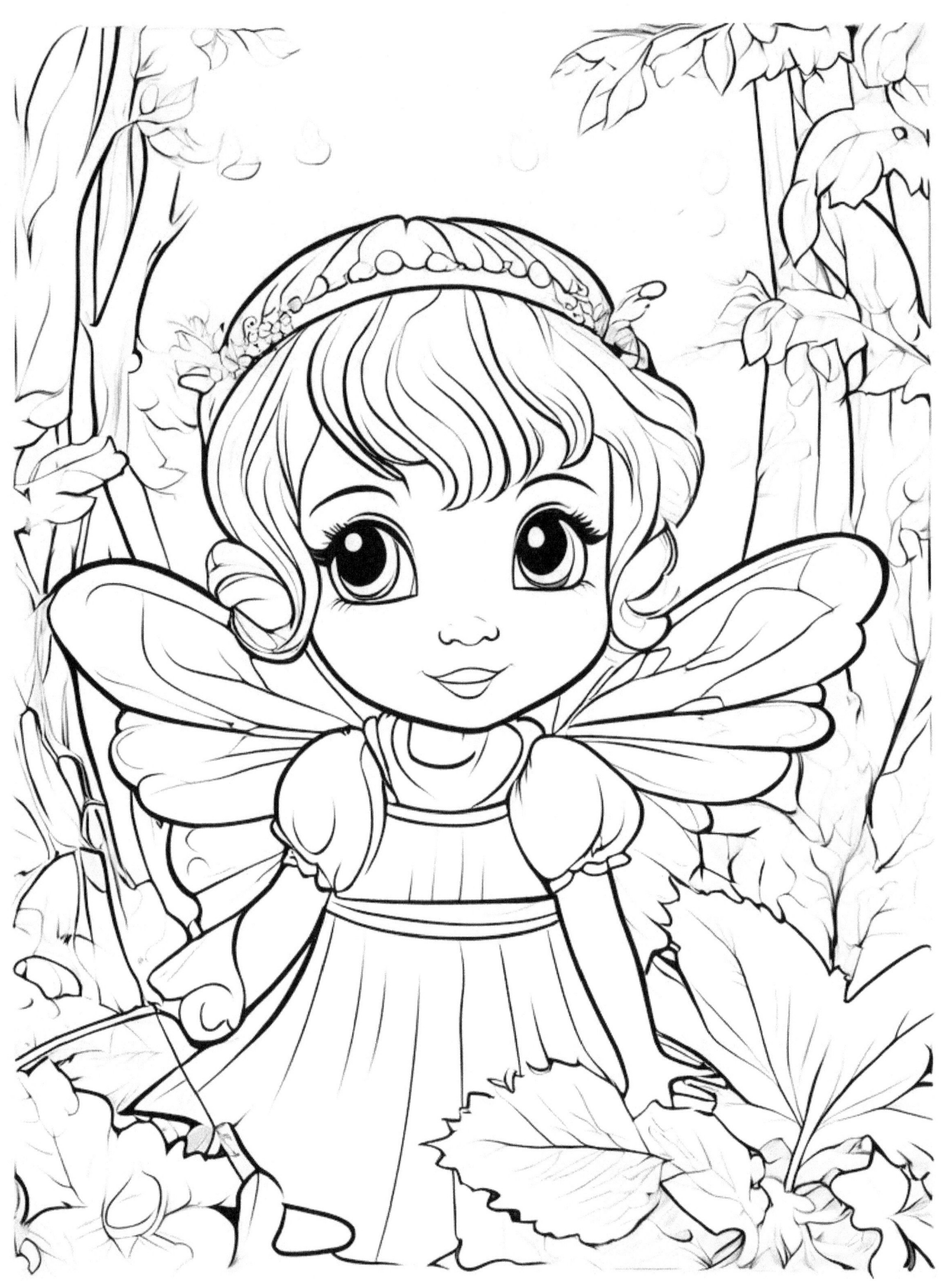

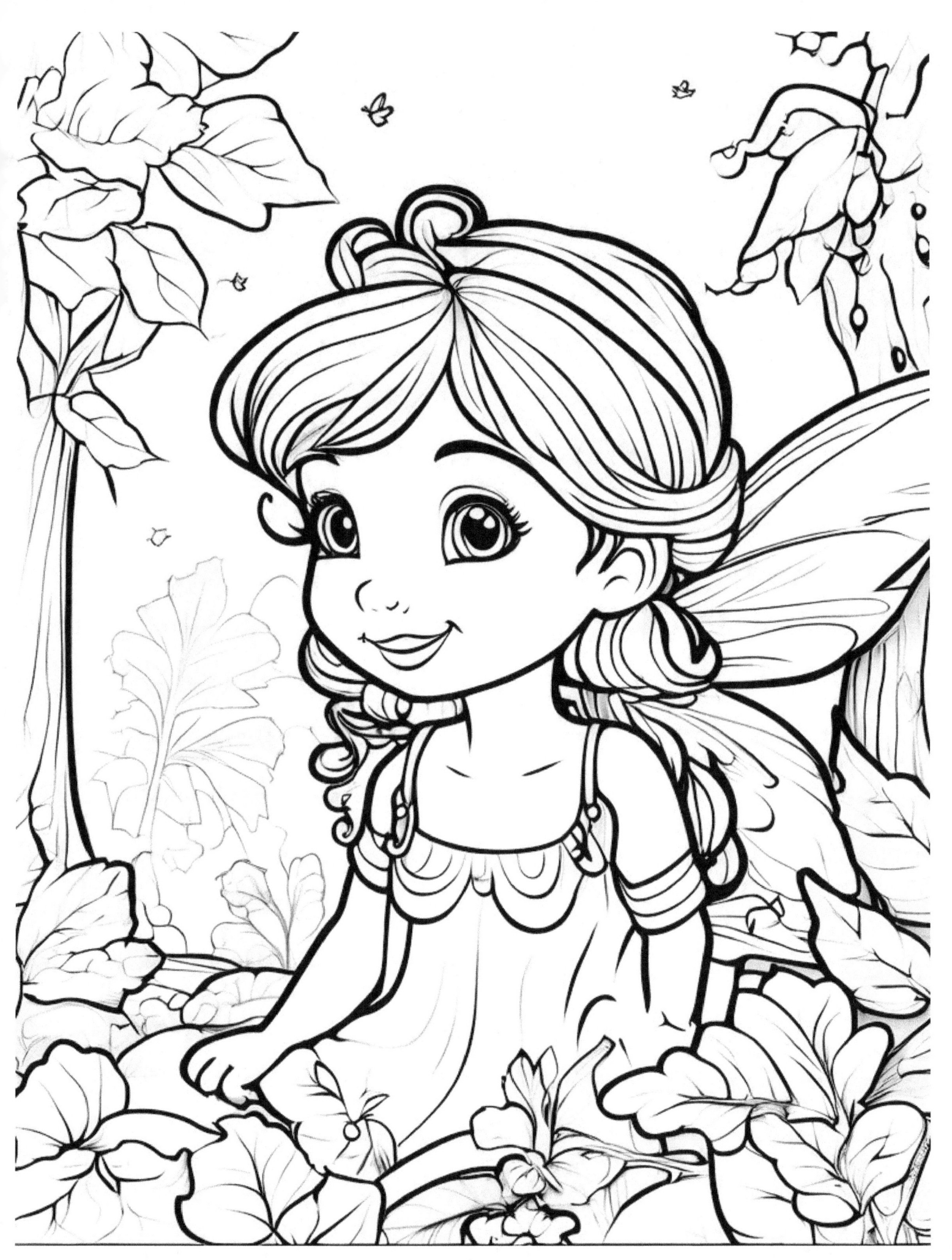

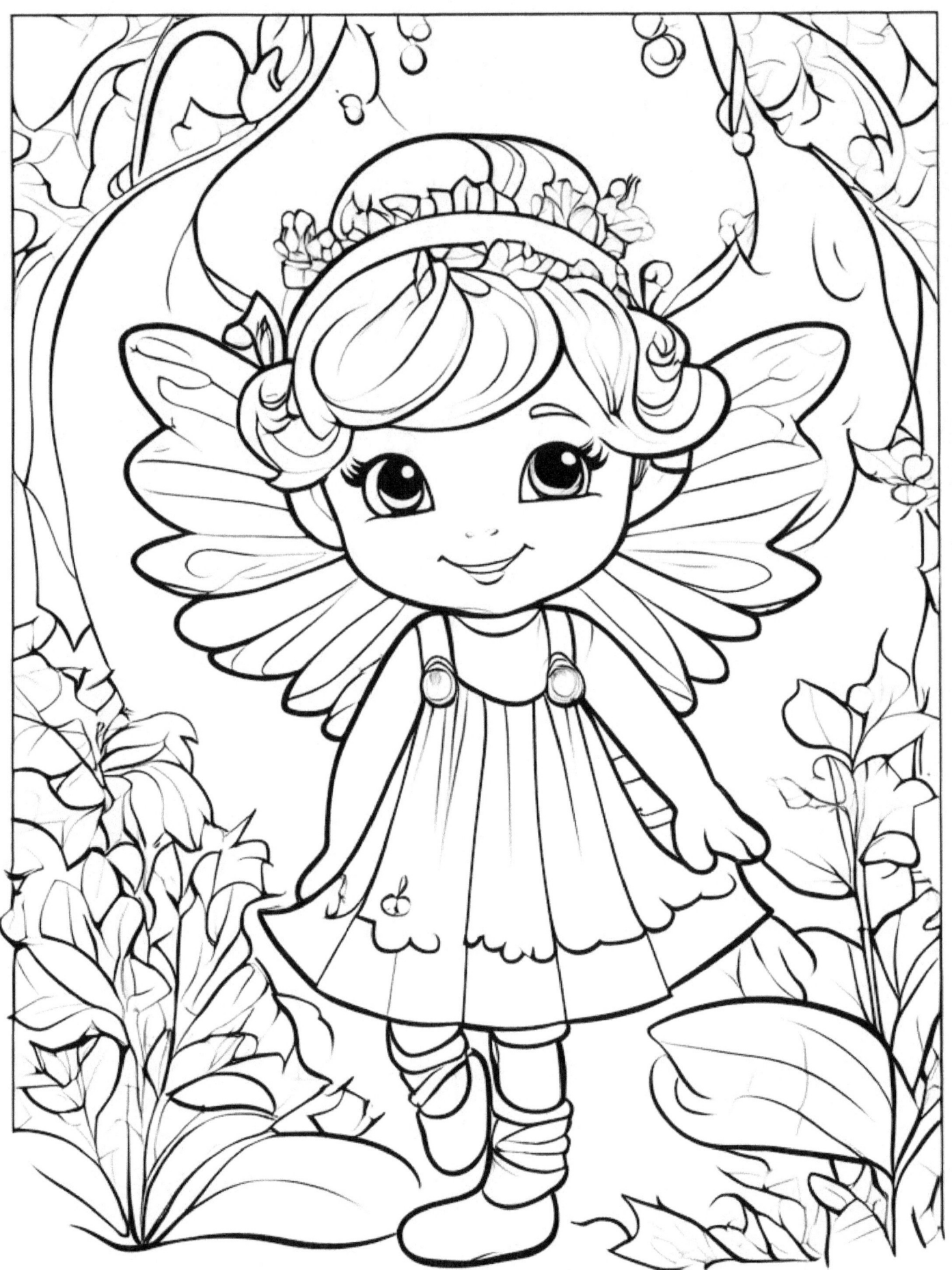

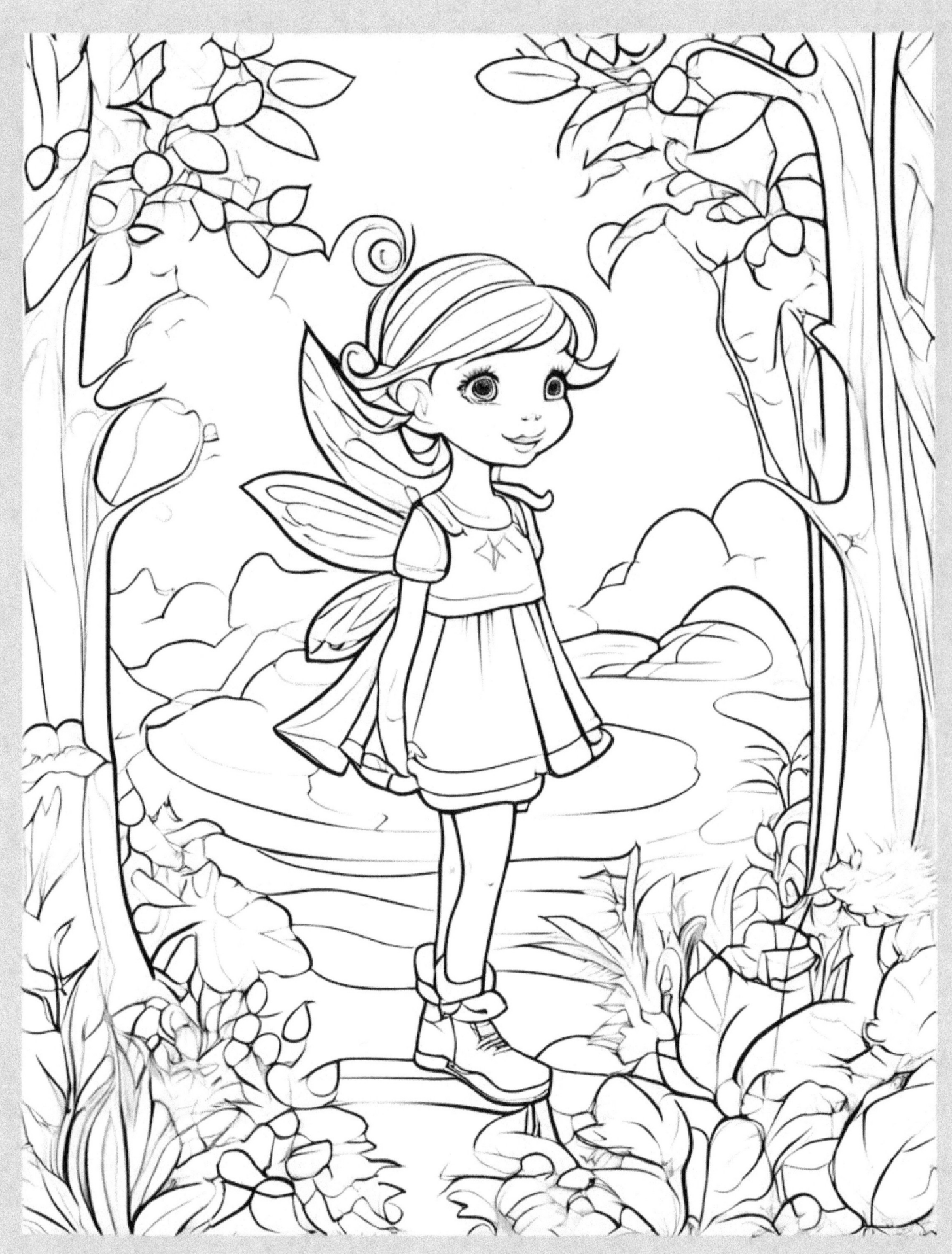

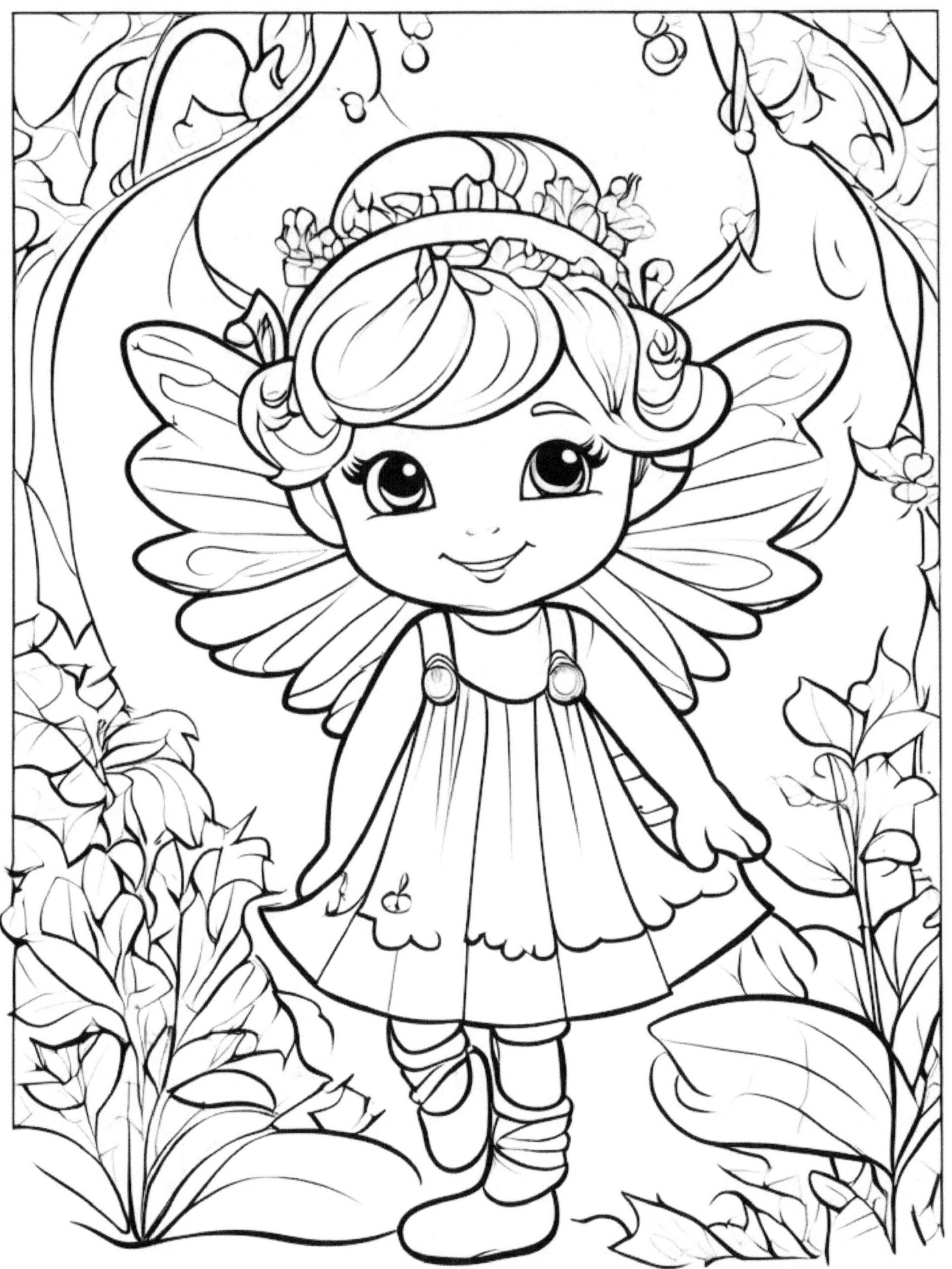

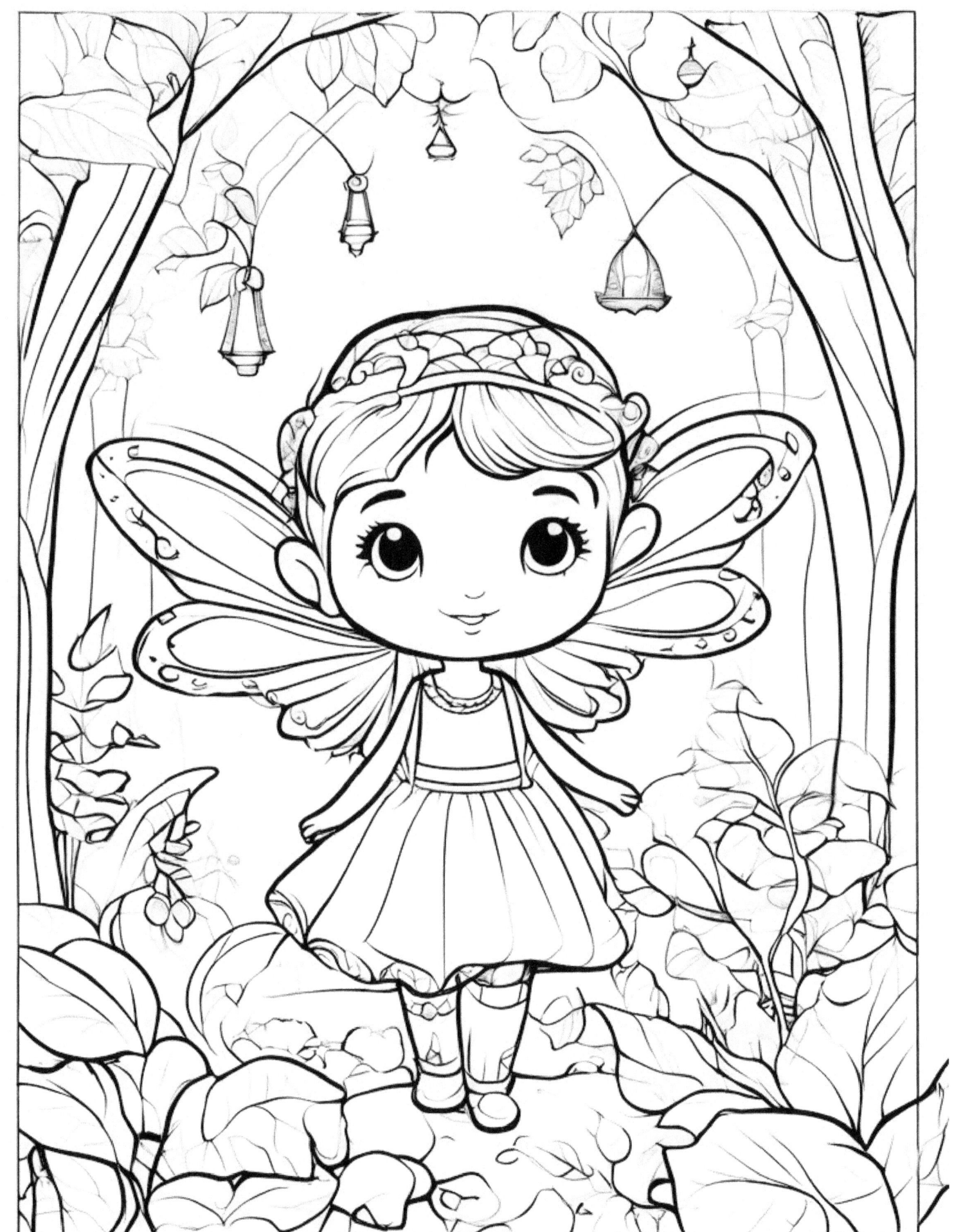

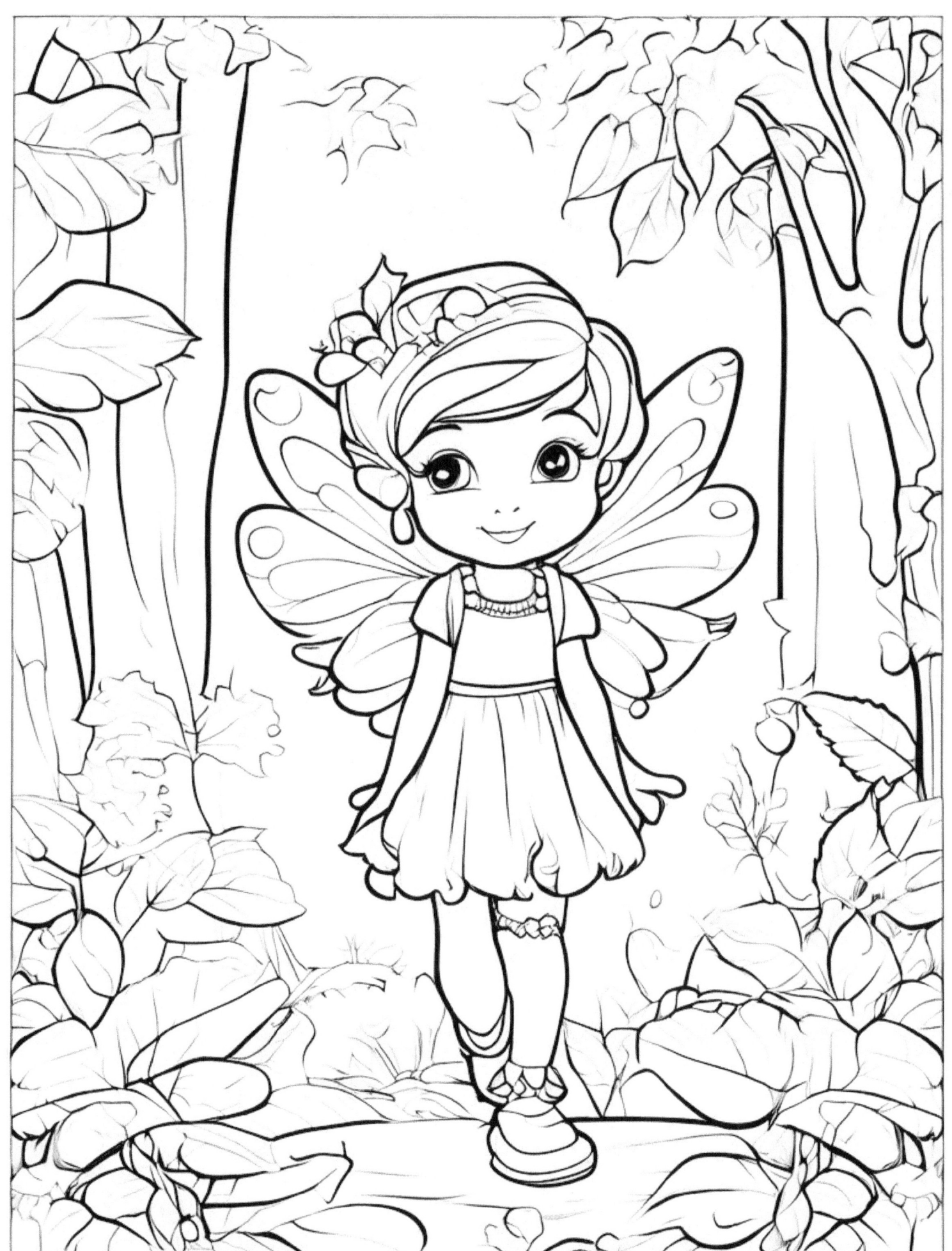

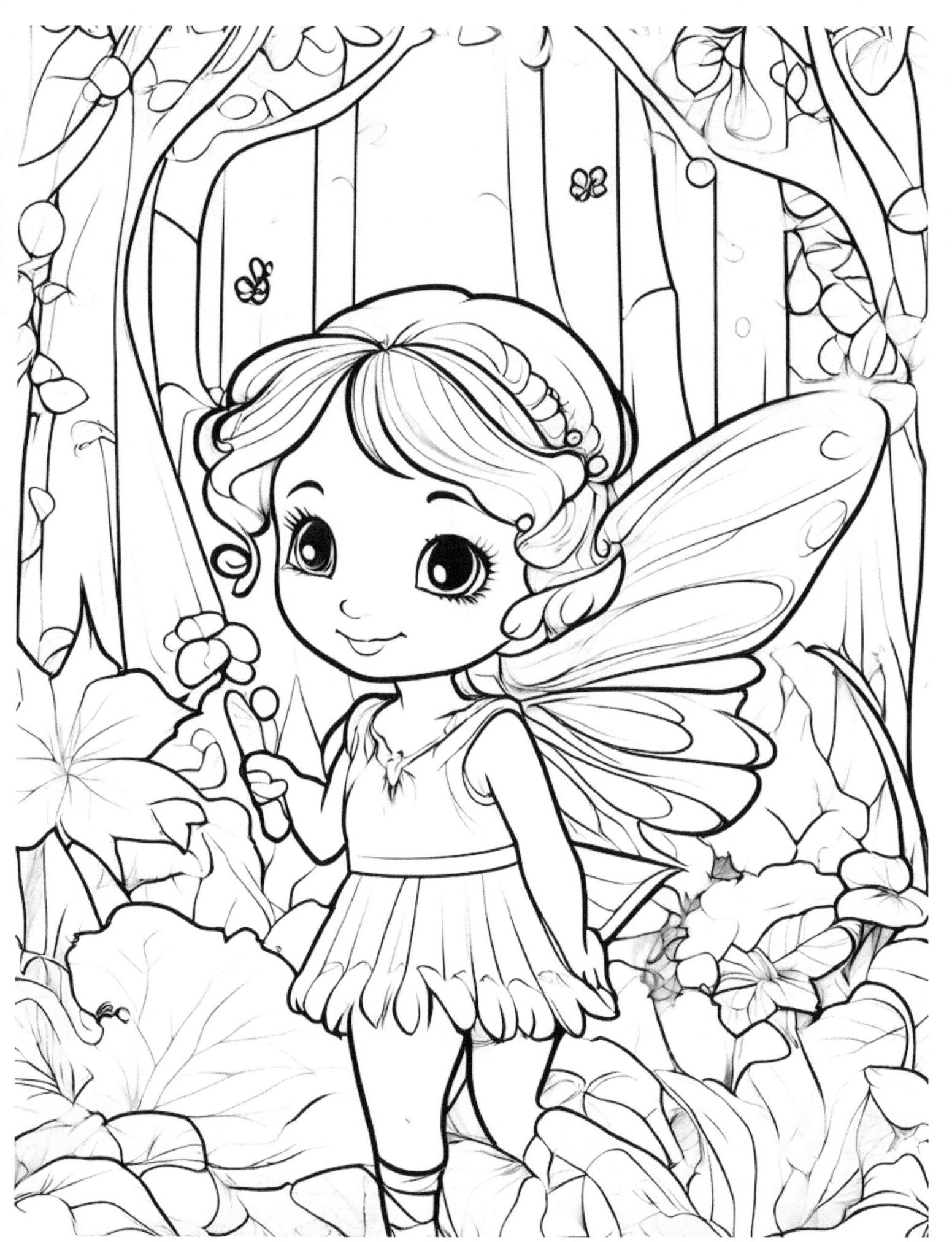

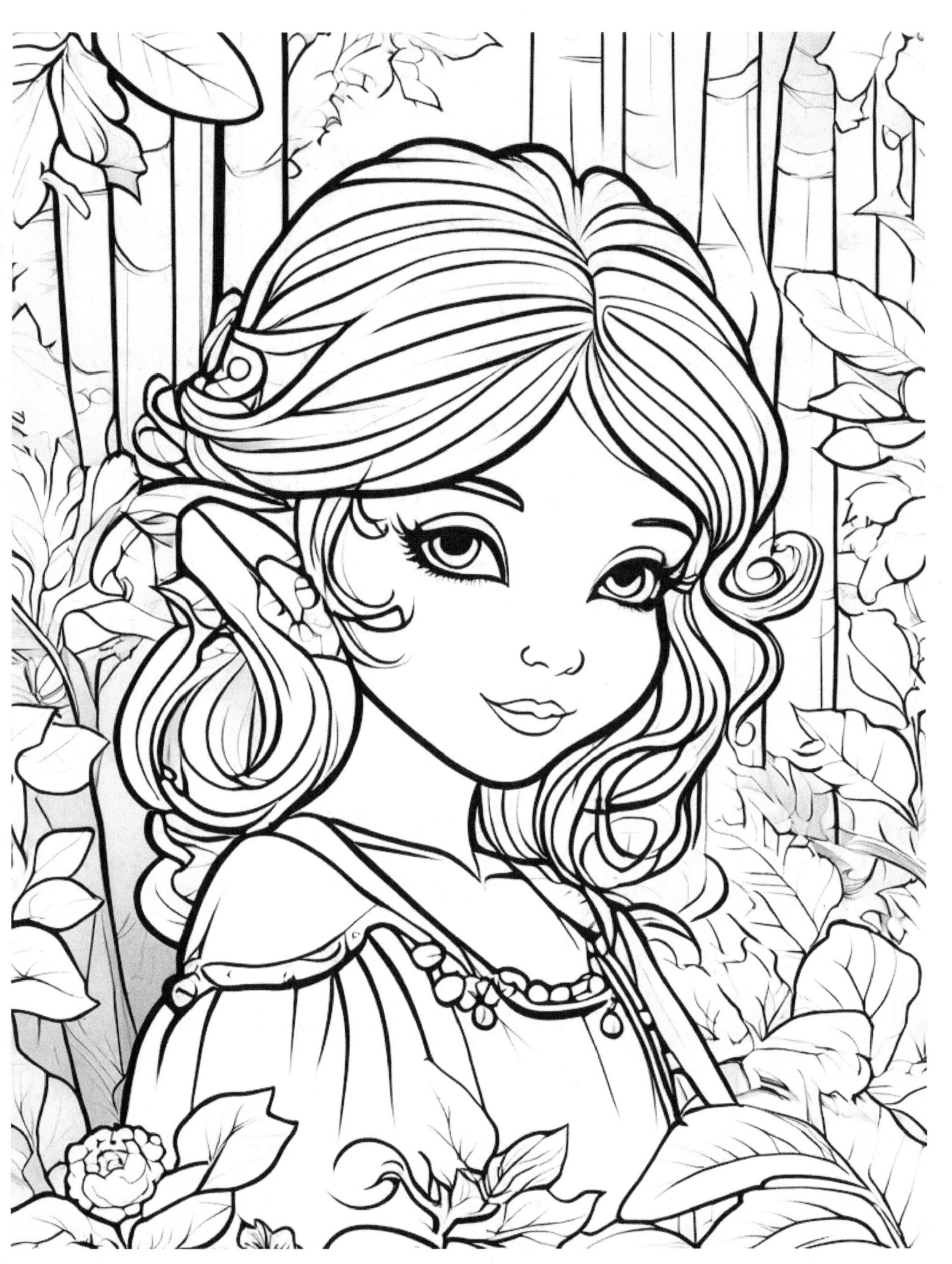

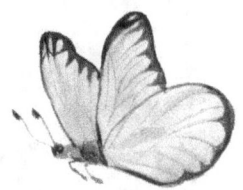

All rights reserved. No part of this coloring book may be reproduced or transmitted in any form or by any means, electronic or mechanical, including photocopying, recording, or any information storage and retrieval system, without permission in writing from the copyright holder, except for personal or educational use. Non-compliance with this restriction may result in civil and criminal penalties. The illustrations in this book are copyrighted and have been created exclusively for the book "Enchanted Fairyland: A Magical Coloring Adventure for Children." Any unauthorized use of the illustrations is strictly prohibited.

CRIS CARDOSO 2024